Racial Trauma in the School System

Racial Trauma in the School System provides foundational and clinical information for school-based mental health professionals to better understand and address the nuanced experience of racial trauma in their school.

The book focuses on conceptualizing racial trauma and the impact it has on a child's development and academic functioning, providing information on how to look at racially based experiences through a trauma-informed lens. Examining a wide range of racial and ethnic identities, chapters explore critical issues such as ethno-racial identity development and diagnostic classifications to help readers develop a conceptual lens to guide their approach. The clinical application of theory to practice is emphasized using complex case studies and the explanation of practical interventions. This text is the first of its kind to focus exclusively on discussing the impact of racial trauma on children and to discuss the intersection between identity and racism in the school system.

Geared toward school-based professionals, this book considers racial trauma across a wide range of contexts and clinical presentations for other mental health professionals to adapt and apply the content to their clinical practice.

Connesia Handford, PsyD, is a Black psychologist working in Austin, Texas. She specializes in addressing Black mental health and racial trauma across the developmental life span.

Ariel D. Marrero, PsyD, is a Latinx psychologist working in the San Francisco Bay Area. She specializes in the intersection between a child's mental health needs and their overall school functioning.

Racial Trauma in the School System

Naming the Pain

CONNESIA HANDFORD
AND ARIEL D. MARRERO

Routledge
Taylor & Francis Group

NEW YORK AND LONDON

First published 2022
by Routledge
605 Third Avenue, New York, NY 10158

and by Routledge
2 Park Square, Milton Park, Abingdon, Oxon, OX14 4RN

Routledge is an imprint of the Taylor & Francis Group, an informa business

Library of Congress Cataloging-in-Publication Data
Names: Handford, Connesia, author. | Marrero, Ariel D., author.
Title: Racial trauma in the school system : naming the pain / Connesia
Handford and Ariel D. Marrero.
Description: New York, NY : Routledge, 2021. | Includes bibliographical
references and index. |
Identifiers: LCCN 2021002561 (print) | LCCN 2021002562 (ebook) |
ISBN 9780367139964 (hbk) | ISBN 9780367139971 (pbk) |
ISBN 9780429029615 (ebk)
Subjects: LCSH: Racism–Psychological aspects. | Race awareness. | Racism
in education. | Child psychology. | Child development.
Classification: LCC BF575.P9 H366 2021 (print) | LCC BF575.P9 (ebook) |
DDC 155.8/2–dc23
LC record available at https://lccn.loc.gov/2021002561
LC ebook record available at https://lccn.loc.gov/2021002562

ISBN: 978-0-367-13996-4 (hbk)
ISBN: 978-0-367-13997-1 (pbk)
ISBN: 978-0-429-02961-5 (ebk)

Typeset in Avenir and Dante
by KnowledgeWorks Global Ltd.

To the children of color who are silently struggling with the pain of an unjust world. We see you. We hear you. Your pain matters.

Contents

Acknowledgments

Connesia Handford

I would like to acknowledge and thank all the individuals I have engaged in racial-trauma work with. I do not take for granted the honor of joining and influencing the mental health journey of those fighting for what they deserve. Thank you for allowing me to witness and grow from your incredible strength and vulnerability. To my parents Phyllis and Connell Sr., siblings Connell Jr., Jonathan, and Janeka, thank you so much for all your support, love, encouragement, and inspiration. To my beautiful nieces Phoenix and Charley, I hope this book helps make your world brighter and better. To my grandmothers Daisy and Helen, you both were epitomes of Black womanhood and I hope I made you proud. A very special thank you to my partner in life Suraju, you truly are the best. Thank you for your unrelenting and unwavering support and help. You are my grounding force in this crazy world and I could not have gotten through this process without you. And most importantly, thank you, Ariel. There is no one I would rather work with on Sundays. Thank you for all your hard work along this wild ride, we did it!

Ariel Marrero

First, I would like to thank the children and families I have had the privilege of working with, as they have served as inspiration for this book. Thank you for inviting me into your world and allowing me to witness your immense strength and resilience. With much love and gratitude, I would also like to thank my family and friends for supporting me through this intense process. From the beginning, you have believed in me and have cheered me on as I have worked toward my dreams. A special thank you to my other half, Billy, for reading drafts, proofreading, and supporting my late nights. I am also grateful for the support of Anne Stewart, who has continuously pushed for my voice to be heard. To Virginia, Carly, and Jay, thank you for the unrelenting support. Finally, a big thank you to Connesia, for being my partner in this crazy process! Thank you for all of the hard work you put in to help make this idea into a reality.

Part One

Conceptual Foundations

What Is Racial Trauma?　1

Introduction

Imagine you're an 11-year-old sitting in math class when you feel a tap on your shoulder. You turn around and your friend asks if you've heard about the woman who was found dead in jail after a routine traffic stop. You say no, so they hand you their phone and you read the story of Sandra Bland. Later in the day, while in the locker room, your gym class gathers around a cellphone to watch the footage of the traffic stop that has been leaked to the media. The kids around you laugh and make comments about how she "should have" acted. You can't take your eyes off the screen; your stomach starts to hurt.

On the bus ride home, you start to think about how much Sandra Bland looks like your mom and your aunt. You start to think about the last time you and your mom were pulled over by police and remember the way her hand shook as she grabbed her license from her purse and told you not to move. Your thoughts are interrupted by the bus driver telling you to get off at your stop. When you get home, you head to your mom's bedroom to talk about the video you saw, but notice she's already left for work. You try to call her, but her phone goes straight to voicemail; your heart starts to beat fast as you imagine what could happen on her way to work. As you transition to doing your homework, you notice you're having trouble focusing and can't remember the lesson from class. When she finally gets home, you feel a mixture of relief and anger. As she starts to check your homework, you start yelling at her about not answering the phone. You're sent to bed where you toss and turn all night. The next morning you're exhausted and fall asleep in math class.

The scenario described above is a reality for many children of color in the United States. Traumatic race-related crimes of the last 10 years have brought the issues of racism and privilege to public awareness. Seeing pictures and videos of racially motivated shootings, immigration raids, and overt hate speech in the media has become the norm. While this widespread exposure to incidents of racism is new, the experience of racism and racial injury is not. Many families of color continue to experience traumatic experiences of racial slurs, hate crimes, physical assaults, and daily microaggressions. While adults have the capacity to make sense of their experiences of race and racism, children often have difficulty processing and articulating negative racial experiences. The explicit and subtle messages from media, family, and peers have the potential to impact a child's identity and behavior before they have the ability to conceptualize what racism is. These negative experiences leave hidden wounds which can scar the psyche and impact a child's journey into adulthood if left unaddressed.

Children typically spend most of their day in an educational setting. On average, children in the United States spend 6.8 hours a day at school, totaling 180 days per year (Education Commission of the States, 2018). As children navigate through K-12 education, they meet countless administrators, nurses, school mental health professionals, teachers, security, custodial staff, paraprofessionals, peers, and parents. Each of these interactions has the potential to imprint a supportive, ambivalent, or oppressive experience in a child's life. For many students, school is a place of safety and security; however, for many students of color, the school setting can be a source of distressing race-based incidents. Racially traumatic experiences at school can add new scars, exacerbate old wounds, and add an additional layer of complexity to a child's experience of the world.

Despite the growing research on racial trauma, many children do not receive clinical treatment that is tailored to healing these hidden wounds. Issues of racism are often kept outside the therapy room, which means that many youth suffer in silence. Due to the nuanced nature of this distress, school-based conceptualizations and interventions should be intentional and reflect an understanding of the student's needs. This can be done across the school system with trauma-informed approaches being adopted by administrators, teachers, school counselors, and school psychologists. This book hopes to provide a pathway for understanding racial trauma from a psychological perspective for school-based mental health professionals. Specifically, this chapter will provide an overview of race-related distress, including definitions, supporting research, and a framework for conceptualizing the spectrum of experiences.

Naming the Pain

What exactly *is* racial trauma? Before introducing racial trauma, it's important to explore the concepts that lie at its core. When discussing issues related to identity, it's important to acknowledge the power of language. Because language can be used as both a tool of inclusion and a tool of oppression, we want to be clear about the terms being used in this book. First, while this book uses the term *race*, it does not represent the rigid Black/white dichotomy that is often used in discussions about race in the United States. Race and ethnicity are different concepts, with race referring to shared physical qualities and ethnicity denoting geographic qualities. However, despite their distinct definitions, race and ethnicity are intertwined when conceptualizing cultural impact on identity development, exposure to negative events, and areas of growth when creating a culturally informed school system. As a result, when this book refers to the impact of an individual's racial identity, it is referring to the impact of the wide range of ethnic and racial identities that can make up an individual's sense of self.

When conceptualizing the outcomes of negative ethno-racial experiences and helping others understand how they may be contributing, one must have an understanding of the terms used to describe the initial triggering stimuli. These experiences, known as negative racial experiences, are the real or perceived interpersonal slights, discrimination, humiliating or shaming events, and threats of harm or injury focused on one's ethno-racial identity (Comas-Diaz, 2016). Negative experiences can come in various forms ranging from covert bias to overt hate crimes. Discrimination, prejudice, and bias are often used interchangeably when discussing interpersonal dynamics. We posit that this is problematic as it denies the inherent power that these terms carry. By interchanging words, one semantically denies the reality of that individual's experience. By understanding the difference between each concept, one will be more equipped to identify, understand, and empathize with the experience of the impacted individual. Bias is the proclivity toward a certain idea. This can influence prejudice, or an unjustified attitude toward or judgment of others. One's prejudice can then manifest as discrimination, which is the unjust or unfair treatment of people of a certain group related to one's bias and prejudice.

Microaggressions, or the everyday behavioral and verbal injustices that send hostile, derogatory, and/or invalidating messages to people of color, are another type of negative racial experience that is seen across environments and amongst all ages (Comas-Diaz, 2016). Microaggressions are often the result of underlying or unconscious bias, which means the perpetrator may be unaware of the hurtful messages that they are sending. However, an incident being identified or treated as a microaggression is not contingent upon the intention of the perpetrator but rather the impact experienced by the victim. For example, while the statement "you are pretty for a dark-skinned girl" may be stated with intent to compliment, the impact of it is likely to be hurtful and reinforce the stereotype that darker skin is ordinarily not attractive. Despite the intent, actions that demonstrate microaggressions, prejudice, and discrimination are imbedded in the context of racism.

Now that we have discussed the language that helps identify negative racial encounters, we must explore the language that helps describe the potential impact of the aforementioned concepts. Again, we come to the question, *what is racial trauma?* We argue that the psychological impact of negative racial encounters exists on a spectrum, ranging from racial injury to racial trauma. On one end lies an individual's internal and/or external distress to the event, known as racial injury. At the other end is racial trauma, or the experience of being psychologically traumatized by the event. It's important to note that because these terms exist on a spectrum, there is no rigid categorical line that separates the two experiences. Nor should one's experience on it be thought of as stagnant for any one event or a series of events. Racial injury and racial trauma can result from encounters experienced directly or vicariously, as an individual or as a collective. As we mentioned earlier, language is important and has the power to alter an individual's narrative of an experience. As such, because the line between racial injury and racial trauma is fluid, we will use the term *racial trauma* to encompass the entire spectrum of potential psychological experiences of negative racial situations. Mental health professionals should in turn use both a cultural and trauma-informed clinical lens to determine where a child's presentation falls on the spectrum and respond accordingly.

Racial trauma can exist at multiple levels: the individual level, group level, community level, and cultural level. Within these levels, the trauma can be experienced directly or indirectly. Indirect racial trauma can be present in the form of cultural or community trauma. This occurs when a trauma is endured within familial, historical, or sociopolitical contexts that elicit discriminatory or violent behavior toward one's racial group membership (Helms et al., 2012). For example, in 2014, when Eric Garner was murdered by the police, the impact was felt throughout Black communities in the United States. At the community level, anger, pain, and confusion fueled discussions and protests as individuals addressed the racial trauma that stemmed from the incident and subsequent trial. On the individual level, many struggled with feelings of hypervigilance, intrusive thoughts, and avoidance. These trauma symptoms are still experienced today as people of color grapple with how their racial identity intersects with safety, cultural worth, and well-being.

As the frequency of negative racial events increases, so does the intensity of the trauma felt. This can then lead to insidious trauma, which people of color may experience as a result of the cumulative and continuous exposure to discriminatory acts that undermine their humanity (Comas-Diaz, 2016). For example, earlier in the section, we described a microaggression associated with darker-colored skin. If someone heard this one time without any other negative statements in their normal routine, it would likely elicit a low level of distress that could be resolved fairly easily. However, if a person encountered derogatory or devaluing statements related to their skin color over and over, day after day, the impact would likely be greater. The multiple levels of racial trauma create a complexity that must be addressed when identifying and conceptualizing effective interventions. As trauma research related to the lived experiences of people of color continues to evolve, it is important to reflect on the work that has created the foundation for topics we will expand on throughout this book.

Empirical Research on Racial Trauma

While the presence of racial trauma within communities of color is not new, the examination of it in empirical literature is, as it has become a topic of academic conversation within the last 20 years. Throughout its history of academic study, the concept has held many names including race-related stress, racist incident-based trauma, and race-based trauma. Initial literature focused on establishing racial trauma as a concept and over time, researchers have deepened the psychological community's understanding of it as a multifaceted, complex trauma with connections to healthcare, education, and law. As this book focuses on the application of research to clinical practice, we felt it was important to pay respect to the research that lies at its conceptual foundation.

In the 1990s, empirical research began to examine the connection between racial identity and health outcomes. During this time, many researchers began to look into potential sociological explanations for differences in self-reported health experiences between Black and white Americans. Many looked into these differences and found that compared to white Americans, Black Americans reported higher levels of psychological distress and lower well-being, yet the impact of race had never been examined (Williams et al., 1997). At this time, a growing number of researchers argued that to understand these differences, the areas of race, discrimination, and racism had to be studied as they were important variables that had been traditionally neglected by empirical study (Cooper, 1993; Cooper et al., 1981; King & Williams, 1995; Williams, 1996). This push led to several studies finding race-related stress to be adversely related to physical health and mental health and a strong predictor of psychiatric symptoms (Williams et al., 1997; Klonoff, et al., 1999).

At the turn of the century, many researchers became motivated to deepen their understanding of the connection between race-related stress and psychiatric symptoms. The question shifted from *does* race-related stress play a role to *what kind* of psychological impact does it have on people of color. During this phase, the scope of race-related psychological research expanded. No longer was race thought of as a Black and white binary as research focused on exploring the experiences of different ethnic and racial group memberships. Studies began to find links between racism, discrimination, and psychiatric symptoms including depression, anxiety, and post-traumatic stress symptoms across other racial and ethnic groups including Latinxs, Asian Americans, and Indigenous Americans (Carter & Forsyth, 2010; Kressin, et al., 2008; Krieger et al., 2005; Loo et al., 2001; Mossakowski, 2003; Noh, et al., 2007; Ramos, et al., 2003; Sellers, et al., 2003). This wave led to the psychological impact of racism being conceptualized as not only distressful, but traumatic. Researchers began to notice a pattern of individuals of color experiencing post-traumatic symptoms of hyper-arousal, re-experiencing, and avoidant behavior after encountering negative racial incidents (Bryant-Davis & Ocampo, 2005; Williams et al., 2018).

Currently, the racial trauma movement is focused on how to intervene. As the many facets of racial trauma are explored, how to translate this research into practice is in demand. As a result, practitioners and theorists have begun to contribute to the research and literature on racial trauma by developing theoretical frameworks, treatment approaches, and assessment tools. Specifically, clinical researchers are highlighting the challenges and limitations of identifying racial trauma using the DSM-5, applying current therapeutic approaches to include the treatment of racial trauma, and crafting new theoretical frameworks and assessment measures to identify, conceptualize, and intervene when working with racial trauma (Bryant-Davis & Ocampo, 2005; Bryant-Davis, 2007; Carter, 2007; Comas-Diaz, 2016; Williams et al., 2018).

Conclusion

The complexity of how racial trauma manifests across the developmental life span and across different settings has influenced the breadth and depth of racial trauma research and practice. Currently, studies are showing the impact of racial trauma on child development and the education system (Kohli et al., 2017; Torres & Santiago, 2017). Our book intends to contribute to the research on the intersection of racial trauma and school-based experiences. By creating a comprehensive guide on how to address racial trauma in school systems, we hope to equip mental health professionals with the tools and confidence to be agents of change for students of color.

References

Bryant-Davis, T. (2007). Healing requires recognition: The case for race-based traumatic stress. *The Counseling Psychologist, 35*(1), 135–143.

Bryant-Davis, T., & Ocampo, C. (2005). Racist incident-based trauma. *The Counseling Psychologist, 33*(4), 479–500.

Carter, R.T. (2007). Racism and psychological and emotional injury: Recognizing and assessing race-based traumatic stress. *The Counseling Psychologist, 35*(13), 13–105.

Carter, R.T., & Forsyth, J. (2010). Reactions to racial discrimination: Emotional stress and help-seeking behaviors. *Psychological Trauma: Theory, Research, Practice, and Policy, 2*(3), 183–191.

Comas-Díaz, L. (2016). Racial trauma recovery: A race-informed therapeutic approach to racial wounds. In A.N. Alvarez, C.T.H. Liang, & H.A. Neville (Eds.), *Cultural, racial, and ethnic psychology book series. The cost of racism for people of color: Contextualizing experiences of discrimination* (pp. 249–272). American Psychological Association.

Cooper, R.S. (1993). Health and the social status of blacks in the United States. *Annals of Epidemiology, 3*, 137–144.

Cooper, R.S., Steinhauer, M., Miller, W., David, R., & Schatzkin, A. (1981). Racism, society, and disease: An exploration of the social and biological mechanisms of differential mortality. *International Journal of Health Services, 11*(3), 389–414.

Education Commission of the States. (2018). 50-state comparison: Instructional time policies [Data file]. https://www.ecs.org/50-state-comparison-instructional-time-policies/

Helms, J.E., Nicolas, G., & Green, C.E. (2012). Racism and ethnoviolence as trauma: Enhancing professional and research training. *Traumatology, 18*(1), 65–74.

King, G., & Williams, D.R. (1995). Race and health: A multi-dimensional approach to African American health. In B.C. Amick, S. Levine, D.C. Walsh, & A. Tarlov (Eds.), *Society and health* (pp. 93–130). Oxford University Press.

Klonoff, E.A., Landrine, H., & Ullman, J.B. (1999). Racial discrimination and psychiatric symptoms among blacks. *Cultural Diversity and Ethnic Minority Psychology, 5*(4), 329–339.

Kohli, R., Pizarro, M., & Nevarez, A. (2017). The "new racism" of K-12 schools: Centering critical research on racism. *Review of Research in Education, 41*, 182–202.

Kressin, N.R., Raymond, K.L., & Manze, M. (2008). Perceptions of race/ethnicity-based discrimination: A review of measures and evaluations of their usefulness for the health care setting. *Journal of Health Care for the Poor and Underserved, 19*, 697–730.

Krieger, N., Smith, K., Naishadham, D., Hartman, C., & Barbeau, E.M. (2005). Experiences of discrimination: Validity and reliability of a self-report measure for the population's health research on racism and health. *Social Science and Medicine, 61*, 1576–1596.

Loo, C.M., Scurfield, R.M., King, D.W., Fairbank, J.A., Ruch, L.O., Adams, L.J., & Chemtob, C.M. (2001). Measuring exposure to racism: Development and validation of a race-related stressor scale (RRSS) for Asian American Vietnam veterans. *Psychological Assessment, 13*(4), 503–520.

Mossakowski, K.N. (2003). Coping with perceived discrimination: Does ethnic identity protect mental health? *Journal of Health and Social Behavior, 44,* 318–330.

Noh, S., Kaspar, V., & Wickrama, K.A.S. (2007). Overt and subtle racial discrimination and mental health: Preliminary findings for Korean immigrants. *American Journal of Public Health, 97,* 1269–1274.

Ramos, B., Jaccard, J., & Guilamo-Ramos, V. (2003). Dual ethnicity and depressive symptoms: Implications of being Black and Latino in the United States. *Hispanic Journal of Behavioral Sciences, 25,* 147–173.

Sellers, R.M., Caldwell, H., Schmeelk-Cone, K.H., & Zimmerman, M.A. (2003). Racial identity, racial discrimination, perceived stress, and psychological distress among African American young adults. *Journal of Health and Social Behavior, 44*(3), 302–317.

Torres, S.A., & Santiago, C.D. (2017). Culture and educational stress and internalizing symptoms among Latino adolescents: The role of ethnic identity. *Journal of Educational and Psychological Consultation, 27*(3), 344–366.

Williams, D.R. (1996). Racism and health: A research agenda. *Ethnicity and Disease, 6,* 1–6.

Williams, D.R., Yu, Y., & Jackson, J.S. (1997). Racial differences in physical and mental health. *Journal of Health Psychology, 2*(3), 335–351.

Williams, M.T., Metzger, I.W., Leins, C., & Delapp, C. (2018). Assessing racial trauma within a DSM-5 framework: The UConn racial/ethnic stress & trauma survey. *Practice Innovations, 3*(4), 242–260.

The Impact of Racial Trauma on Identity Development

2

Introduction

When conceptualizing a child's experience in a school system, we first have to establish an understanding of that child's experience of themselves. A child's identity development is a complex process that is heavily influenced by environmental factors, such as the school environment in which they spend most of their time. So, what is identity and how does it develop? Identity is defined as the self's narrative about itself (Shealy, 2016). It is how we understand who and why we are, how we articulate that to ourself and others, and how we navigate our relationship with ourself, others, and the world. Therefore, identity development is merely the process by which our narration is formed. An optimal or ideal identity development is a process in which one's understanding of themselves elicits an experience of fulfillment, competence, relatedness, and autonomy. "Who am I and why?" are the questions that we all strive to answer in our lives. As children, we are collecting the data to remedy those questions and articulate the answers to others.

School plays an intricate role in the identity development process. Both home and school represent systems of socialization that can foster or rupture optimal and healthy identity development for a child. School systems are merely a plethora of developed and developing identities interacting with each other. If teachers, administrators, and staff want a harmonious and well-functioning school environment, they should be in tune with and concerned about the identity development of their students. Mental health professionals working with children should also be invested in collecting information about how a child is experiencing school. A student's perspective and understanding of how and why they are experiencing certain encounters at school will certainly impact any distress they feel and subsequent therapy interventions.

There are many aspects of one's identity and many different dynamics that impact each aspect. America has a long history of racializing individuals and ascribing meaning, rationalization, and action based on this particular type of othering. As a result, ethno-racial membership is a salient part of identity formation for children of color (Umaña-Taylor et al., 2014). This is especially true when distress stems from negative racial encounters. In order to appropriately understand and address a child's experience of race-related distress, one would need to conceptualize where they are in their ethno-racial identity development. As a child spends most of their time in school, being aware of relevant encounters and influences experienced at school is necessary in conceptualizing a child's ethno-racial identity development. Who a child is and how they experience that are two significant psychological ideals. How is a school helping or hurting a child's navigation of these wonderings and is the school mindful or intentional about their role? Ultimately to address racial trauma in the school system is to know how different stages of identity development are experiencing the school's culture as it relates to ethno-racial dynamics and then use that information to tailor change.

Ethno-Racial Identity Development

Ethno-racial identity development is our self-narrative about what it means to be a person of a specific ethno-racial group membership. It is greatly impacted by the beliefs and experiences we are exposed to growing up. As research about racial trauma emerges, so does research related to ethno-racial identity. In 2014, a group of scholars named the *Ethnic and Racial Identity in the 21st Century Study Group* created and published the Ethnic and Racial Identity (ERI) model to explore and conceptualize the ethnic and racial identity development stages for youth of color. They define ERI as "a multidimensional, psychological construct that reflects the beliefs and attitudes that individuals have about their ethnic-racial group memberships, as well as the processes by which these beliefs and attitudes develop over time" (Umaña-Taylor et al., 2014, p. 23). Each developmental stage of the ERI model consists of content, or "the attitudes and beliefs about one's group and its relation to other groups" and process, or "the mechanisms by which individuals explore, form, and maintain their ERI" (Umaña-Taylor et. al, 2014, p. 24). In other words, content is someone's narration of themselves and process is how that narration came to be.

Within the focus of this book, content is the internalized attitudes and beliefs a student of color has about their ethno-racial identity in the school system and process is how those attitudes and beliefs are explored, formed, and maintained in the school system. A school should be a place that fosters expansive and inclusive positive exploration but far too often it is a place where negative and/or confusing ideas are thrust upon children and their identity formation. School experiences directly impact how a child navigates their ERI development and what processes lead to internalized content. Mental health professionals who desire to be agents of change within school systems are tasked with figuring out how to educate teachers, staff, and administrators on how the school is worsening or enriching a student's ERI development.

The ERI model conceptualizes early childhood, middle childhood, adolescence, and emerging adulthood. During early childhood, a child is experiencing differentiation of self and others. This time of realizing that everyone is different elicits the process of attempting to make sense of the differences. Children use assimilation, accommodation, and refinement to make sense of ethno-racial differences (Umaña-Taylor et al., 2014). Through this process, ethnic labeling of themselves occurs as well as an understanding of how to label others. Information about ethno-racial membership, theirs and others, is refined until the child develops ethnic constancy, or an idea of what ethno-racial related knowledge seems dependable and constant to them. A significant amount of the ethno-racial information children collect to assimilate, accommodate, and refine is gathered at school. As a result, we can start to understand how even in early childhood, school starts to mold a child's identity development as they are introduced to peers and adults who are different than their family at home.

Middle childhood marks a time when children become more aware that the aforementioned ethno-racial labels or categorizations garner different amounts of attention, popularity, resources, etc. Awareness of bias and understanding of social hierarchy are the processes that shape this developmental stage (Umaña-Taylor et al., 2014). Within a school context, a student's awareness that peers or adults might assume things about them before actually getting to know them and that people of certain ethno-racial groups will have different social interactions begins to increase during this time. These processes lead the child to form feelings about their ethno-racial group membership. Content formed during this time includes salience, centrality, affect, and public regard (Umaña-Taylor et al., 2014). Salience refers to how significant an individual's ethno-racial membership is to them in particular situations, while centrality is how important that group membership is to their idea of self in general. Affect refers to an understanding of whether one's ethno-racial identity evokes positive or negative emotions for the individual. Or in other words, it is how you feel about your own ethno-racial group membership. If affect is an internal experience, public regard is the external counterpart. Public regard is how a person feels that others and the world experience their ethno-racial group. From a school perspective, this time is crucial as students start to make meaning of their perceived positionality in the classroom and amongst peers.

During adolescence, a child's development is shaped by the molding of the ethno-racial related information they have been gathering. Processes, such as contestation, elaboration, and negotiation are prevalent during this time (Umaña-Taylor et al., 2014). The exploration phase at this time ideally consists of the child engaging in thought, discussion, and activities surrounding their ethno-racial group. This journey of wonder, inquiry, and knowledge gathering prompts a child to dispute, develop, and alter their pre-existing connotations related to their ethno-racial group membership as they incorporate new information. This allows them to determine what values they want to internalize as well as how accepted they feel by others in their ethno-racial group. These processes elicit more internalized attitudes and beliefs around public regard, affect, salience, centrality, and ideology. During this time an individual starts to learn more about shared experiences among members of the same ethno-racial group that differ from others. All this content can result in complex feelings or incidents of certainty, or solidified conviction and comfort with one's ethno-racial membership, and/or identity self-denial which is the distancing or diminishing of one's ethno-racial background (Umaña-Taylor et al., 2014).

The last ERI developmental stage is emerging adulthood. This stage is a deeper continuation of the process and content experienced during adolescence. This time is marked by an increased awareness of all the different aspects of one's identity. Compartmentalizing decreases and one's understanding of themselves ethno-racially, politically, socially, gender wise, career wise, religiously, as well as many other identity markers began to merge and impact each other. This intersectionality results in an ERI that is integrated with other self-concept domains to form one's holistic identity (Umaña-Taylor et al., 2014).

How Racial Trauma Impacts a Child's Ethno-Racial Identity Development

Ideally, an achieved or adaptively developed ethno-racial identity is one in which the individual has actively sought out and gathered information related to their ethno-racial group membership. That information is then filtered to create an internalized narrative of their ethno-racial experience that yields informed articulation, intentional expression, and fulfillment when used to navigate and experience themselves, others, and the world (Handford, 2020). However, when children experience negative racial encounters, they are vulnerable to their ethno-racial identity development becoming less and less optimal, adaptive, and enriching. Racial trauma negatively impacts the processes and content described above. Within the school environment, there are many experiences that can impact significant content in a way that transforms the internal trajectory of a student of color.

For example, students of color are often told they cannot do something because of their ethno-racial membership: "Black people don't play lacrosse," "You thought the math test was hard … but you're Asian?!" "Can you bring a normal lunch sometime?" After a while the constant limitations thrust upon students have the potential to skew their perception of their ethno-racial membership. In those incidents, the salience they experience related to their ethno-racial membership is not a reason for celebration but rather a trigger for psychological distress. The affect they experience becomes more and more negative as moments of positive affirmation and group esteem are not demonstrated or created. Negative racial encounters increase identity self-denial. Even if a child of color has a high sense of certainty, they may minimize their ethno-racial group membership at school for fear that they will be made to feel rejected or dismissed.

Conclusion

So, what does all of this mean for mental health professionals? To understand any child you work with, you need to understand their stages of development and how certain systems are impacting these maturation phases. A child's ethno-racial identity development process and content impact the centrality, or severity, a negative racial encounter poses. As the child spends most of their day at school, a significant portion of their ethno-racial identity development occurs at school or in response to school happenings. Schools have the ability to foster both protective and risk factors for optimal ethno-racial identity development. It can be a place that creates racial trauma or a place that fosters posttraumatic growth. Therefore, a mental health professional would need to understand how racial trauma is impacting a child's ethno-racial identity development and discern the school's role in that before conceptualizing how best to intervene and help the child and the school at large.

References

Handford, C. R. (2020). *Naming the pain: A model and method for therapeutically assessing the psychological impact of racism* [Doctoral dissertation, James Madison University]. JMU Scholarly Commons.

Shealy, C.N. (2016). The EI self: Real world implications and applications of EI theory. In C.N. Shealy (Ed.), *Making sense of beliefs and values: Theory, research, and practice* (1st ed.) (pp. 93–111). Springer Publishing Company.

Umaña-Taylor, A.J., Lee, R.M., Rivas-Drake, D., Syed, M., Seaton, E., Quintana, S.M., Cross, W.E., Schwartz, S.J., & Yip, T. (2014). Ethnic and racial identity during adolescence and into young adulthood: An integrated conceptualization. *Child Development*, 85(1), 21–39.

Culture in the School System

3

Introduction

A student's experience of the school system can have a powerful impact on their developmental trajectory. To put it shortly, perception matters. Perceiving school as a safe space where one is supported, challenged, guided, and most importantly, protected, is one of the most important protective factors for positive academic and mental health outcomes (Wang & Degol, 2016). Those who view the education system as unsafe, unsupportive, or untrustworthy, tend to struggle with engagement, motivation, and connectedness, which can contribute to worse outcomes. For some, this results in truancy issues while for others, it can reinforce the school-to-prison pipeline.

Institutional Racism

The United States education system has a long and complicated history of failing to meet the needs of students of color. While practices have improved, it is important to acknowledge the historical roots in racist and oppressive educational practices. From the forced assimilation of Indigenous children in white boarding schools, to the outlawing of teaching Black children to read and write, the US education system has been a place where students of color have been dehumanized, neglected, and damaged by the policies created by white school administrators. While the civil rights movement helped to eliminate segregation, reduce funding discrimination, and improve the overall treatment of families of color in schools, problems continued. Institutional racism that was once overt has now become covert.

While this subtle form of discrimination is harder to detect, it continues to exist in the US education system. Racist policies and practices reduce the power, privileges, and rights of students of color while communicating messages of inferiority and a lack of belonging (Huber et al., 2006). For many families of color, the education system continues to be a place where they feel unwanted, misunderstood, and targeted. Experiences that contribute to these feelings can range from daily microaggressions from teachers to being discouraged from participating in certain experiences due to skin color.

From a systemic perspective, it is important to highlight how institutional racism is maintained in schools. Larger societal attitudes about race, inequality, power, and privilege influence the type of funding afforded to schools,

---

Case Example: Xiomara

Xiomara is a 17-year-old Afro-Latinx student in the 11th grade who was referred to the school counselor for anger management for displaying "aggressive and inappropriate behavior" in the classroom. Teachers reported that Xiomara is argumentative, defiant, and has difficulty forming relationships with adults and peers. Recently, she received 3 days of in-school suspension for yelling at a substitute teacher, pouring her water bottle on a peer, and walking out the classroom. Her school file indicates that last year Xiomara and her family moved to the rural district in central Pennsylvania from the Bronx. It also highlights that at her previous school she had no disciplinary incidents, was on honor roll, and was described by her teachers as "a pleasant and outspoken student."

Xiomara is placed in a 6-week anger management lunch group that appeared to have little success. During the group, she was quiet, minimally participated, and rolled her eyes at the counselor. During the post-group interview, Xiomara commented, "This wasn't helpful. You just don't get it. I'm angry for a good reason." When the counselor attempted to understand what Xiomara meant, she angrily said, "You wouldn't understand" and walked out of the office. At a parent-teacher meeting the following week, her parents were confused as her behavior is different at home. They explained that at home, Xiomara is respectful and kind but spends the majority of her time in her bedroom.

Xiomara's case will be continued throughout the chapter. As you read on, consider the following questions for reflection:

- How do you understand Xiomara and her behavior?
- What are your treatment recommendations?
- Is a community referral needed? Why or why not?
- What additional information would you like to know?

which impacts the type of resources, materials, and supports for the students (Huber et al., 2006). This lack of resources and supports impacts the policies and practices that are put in place at the school, which influences the beliefs and behaviors of the administrators, teachers, and staff. For example, if a predominantly Black high school receives less funding than the predominantly white high school due to test scores, that school will have less resources available to educate the students. With less funding for important "extras" such as mental health programming, college and career programming, and community outreach, this predominantly Black school may utilize harsher more punitive practices that reinforce racist societal attitudes. These attitudes can negatively impact the school climate which can result in biased, racist, and oppressive interactions between school personnel and the individual students (and their families).

Day-to-Day Battle Wounds

Racial battle fatigue is a term created by Smith (2004) to conceptualize the stress, psychological harm, and physiological distress that people of color can experience when faced with chronic racism, prejudice, and discrimination in an educational setting. It has most notably been applied to the experience of Black educators and college students in the post-secondary education system. Smith argued that the increased dropout rates for Black male college students can be viewed as a function of racial battle fatigue rather than academic preparedness due to the cumulative racial discrimination embedded in the environment (Smith, 2004; Smith et al., 2011). This framework highlights the connection between educational environment, psychological distress, and academic performance for students of color and can be applied to K-12 education. If students of color are burdened with an educational environment that is discriminatory, hostile, and unwelcoming, over time, their distress will have a negative impact on their academic performance.

What types of experiences contribute to racial battle fatigue for students of color? For many students, battle wounds are created by daily instances of covert racism that are hidden in their educational experience. A qualitative study by Call-Cummings and Martinez (2017) featured Latinx students discussing their experience of microaggressions from white teachers and how it contributed to their racial battle fatigue. The students highlighted experiences such as educators' lack of understanding of covert racism and a refusal to acknowledge racism in the classroom that contributes to a cycle of oppression that results in distress (Call-Cummings & Martinez, 2017). For these students, each day they entered the school they were faced with distressing experiences caused by interpersonal teacher-student interactions that made them feel different from white students and unwelcome in the classroom.

Mistreatment of Names

K-12 education research has highlighted how many students of color experience daily microaggressions by teachers, administrators, and fellow students, that contribute to cumulative psychological distress (Huber et al., 2006). One type of microaggression that is well documented is the mistreatment of the names of students of color. A child's name is important as it is tied to their identity, self-concept, and cultural history (Kohli & Solorzano, 2012). For many students, when they go to school their name is mispronounced, made fun of, and sometimes even changed for convenience. Many teachers rationalize this practice by exclaiming that the names are hard to pronounce and assign nicknames while others feel uncomfortable with their inability to correctly pronounce the name and simply avoid using the student's name. It's important to highlight that this microaggression is rooted in the historical practice of renaming enslaved Africans and Indigenous Americans that was prevalent in the 17th through 19th centuries (Kohli & Solorzano, 2012). While forced naming practices have ended, this covert form of discrimination has remained.

For students of color, this experience can send the message that they are unwelcome, that their presence is an inconvenience, and that they do not belong in the classroom. A study by Kohli and Solorzano (2012) examined the impact of chronic name mispronunciation and found that participants described a cultural othering contributing to feelings of disrespect, humiliation, and invisibility. Most concerning, participants identified an impact of internalized racism that resulted from their chronic experiences (Kohli & Solorzano, 2012). For these individuals this daily experience negatively shifted the way they viewed themself and their cultural identity (Huber et al., 2006). For some participants, the embarrassment, shame, and distress were so severe that they disregarded their original names and adopted more Americanized names to get relief (Kohli & Solorzano, 2012). This highlights how the mistreatment of names, which can seem insignificant to some, when experienced on a daily basis, can leave battle wounds on the student's psyche that extend into adulthood.

Expectations and Stereotypes

The expectations and stereotyped beliefs that school personnel have toward certain groups of students can also lead to harmful daily interpersonal interactions. In the United States, the achievement gap between white students and minority students is well documented. In general, Black and Latinx students tend to score lower on achievement tests than their European American and Asian American counterparts (Chang & Demyan, 2007; McKown & Weinstein, 2008; Van den Bergh et al., 2010). One variable that has been proposed as a contributor to this achievement gap is teacher expectation (McKown & Weinstein, 2008). Specifically, the expectations that teachers have about the achievement capabilities of certain ethnic groups influence the way they behave toward them.

When teachers have biased beliefs about race and ethnicity, they can form prejudicial expectations that negatively influence how they run their classroom and treat their students. Implicit racial bias among K-12 teachers has been highlighted in research. Many studies have found that teachers will grade students differently and hold different expectations about achievement based on the student's ethno-racial identity (Bonefeld & Dickhauser, 2018, McKown & Weinstein, 2008). Furthermore, teachers tend to view Asian students as academically successful, cooperative, and having few behavioral problems, while having lower expectations of Black students' academic ability and viewing them as more disruptive (Chang & Demyan, 2007). These biased beliefs are in line with the educational stereotypes of Black students as the troublemaker and Asian American students as the model minority (Chang & Demyan, 2007).

These stereotypes and expectations contribute to microaggressions, microinequities, and prejudicial student–teacher interactions. Microinequities are defined by Sue et al. (2007) as "a pattern of being overlooked, under-respected, and devalued because of one's race or gender" (p. 273). Educational research has found that teachers tend to provide Black students with higher rates of negative verbal feedback, are given less attention in the classroom, and are ignored more often, even if they are identified as gifted (Chang & Demyan, 2007). Teachers have also been found to use more positive and neutral speech with European American students than with ethnic minority students (Tenenbaum & Ruck, 2007).

These daily behavioral patterns send students negative messages about their worth, their intelligence, their value, and their acceptance in the classroom. For example, many Black college students have identified feeling invisible, receiving differential treatment, and feel stereotyped in the classroom

(Solorzano et al., 2000). These experiences have also been documented in Black high school students. A study by Allen (2010) examined the schooling experiences of Black middle-class males in Arizona secondary schools and found that they identified similar feelings of invisibility and differential treatment from teachers. Specifically, they reported that teachers and administrators did not take enough time to get to know them or have meaningful interactions with them (Allen, 2010). They also described being treated differently from their white and Latinx peers on issues related to discipline as their school administrators demonstrated their distrust for Black students (Allen, 2010) Overall, the men in the study felt undervalued and deemed unimportant by school teachers and administrators due to the day-to-day microaggressions they experienced.

Stereotype Threat

When students are placed in an environment that is flooded with negative messages about their identity, worth, and perceived success, it can have a noticeable impact on their school-related behavior. For some students, the constant exposure to microaggressions and teacher bias can contribute to poor academic performance and increased behavioral difficulty in the classroom. This is representative of a normative trauma response to chronic toxic stress. While this will be discussed more in-depth in the next chapter, it is important to highlight how this exposure is related to another reality for many students of color: stereotype threat.

Often, parents and educators become confused as they perceive students as acting in ways that align with their teacher's biased expectations. This can lead to the question, why do some students behave or perform in ways that reinforce these negative beliefs? Stereotype threat refers to the social-psychological phenomenon of being at risk of conforming with negative stereotypes about one's identity group (Aronson et al., 2002; Osborne, 2001). This often occurs in situations where the stereotype is most relevant. For example, as described above, many Black students receive messages from educators that they are intellectually inferior and are not expected to perform as high as other students. Thus, when placed in situations where intellectual ability is relevant, such as during a test or speaking in class, some Black students have an extra cognitive and emotional burden which disrupts their performance and increases anxiety about confirming the stereotype (Aronson et al., 2002). Each student handles this increased burden and anxiety differently. One student may become so anxious that they struggle to remember what they have learned and flunk the test while another student may wish to avoid the source of the anxiety, resulting in a behavioral outburst which sends them to the principal's office. In both examples, their performance and behavior inadvertently reinforce their teacher's biased beliefs about their racial group.

This complex, unconscious phenomenon highlights an additional burden that students of color can carry when navigating the complicated world of education. Educational research has found that overall, students of color demonstrate more anxiety during academic performance than white students and this anxiety extends into college (Aronson et al., 2002; Osborne, 2001). In addition to the increased anxiety, another way that stereotype threat can impact the student is through disidentification. Disidentification refers to

---

Case Example: Xiomara

A week after Xiomara's incident with the counselor, the school psychologist decides to observe her in the classroom to gather data on her disruptive behavior. Throughout the day, the psychologist begins to notice that each teacher has a different nickname for her: one calls her by her middle name (Gabriella), another calls her Zo, and a third teacher calls her by a shortened version of her last name. The psychologist also notes that each time this happens Xiomara tenses, clenches her jaw, and her peers laugh. In English, the teacher is discussing college application essays and makes an offhand comment "some of you won't have to worry about college essays" while looking at Xiomara. The psychologist notices that after this comment she asks to go to the bathroom and skips the remainder of the class period.

At the end of the week, the psychologist calls Xiomara down to his office and explains who he is and his role in the school. He explained that when he observed her in the classroom, he noticed that each teacher called her a different name. She rolled her eyes, folded her arms, and commented "Yeah apparently my name makes people uncomfortable." The psychologist also explained how he heard the comment her English teacher made about college essays. Xiomara's eyes widened briefly and replied, "You caught that? She says things like that all the time. She doesn't like me...no one here does. They're just waiting for me to drop out or get kicked out."

Reflection Questions

- Has your conceptualization of Xiomara changed after receiving additional information? If so, how has it changed?
- What do you think she needs?
- What levels of intervention are needed in this situation?

a disengagement with achievement that helps a student cope with the stress of stereotypes and underperformance (Aronson et al., 2002). Negative experiences in the school environment can hurt a student's sense of self and overall self-esteem. When disidentification happens, after a negative experience, a student disengages with a particular domain of academics in an attempt to protect self-esteem. For example, if a student is told that they are lazy and do not put in enough effort, they may initially push back and refuse to engage. While this process starts off as temporary, if faced with continual negative experiences over time, it can lead to a permanent disengagement. This is concerning as reduced identification can act as a serious barrier to long-term academic achievement.

Overrepresentation in Special Education

Racial bias is also seen across school districts with the overrepresentation of students of color in the special education system. While rates vary by state, Indigenous and Black students tend to be significantly more likely to become eligible for special education services. Black students are twice as likely to be classified as emotionally disturbed and having an intellectual disability, while Indigenous students are almost 1.5 times more likely to be classified as having a specific learning disability (Ahram et al., 2011). Interestingly, Latinx students' rates of special education classifications vary wildly by state, alternating between being underrepresented and overrepresented (Ahram et al., 2011; Togut, 2011). These rates are concerning as the over-identification and misplacement of students of color can reinforce negative stereotypes, place limitations on educational trajectories, and lead to further stigmatization from adults and systems. Additionally, research highlights poorer outcomes for Black students in special education including increased segregated special education placements, reduced access to the general education classroom, and higher dropout rates (Blanchett, 2006). Several factors that have contributed to this disproportionality for students of color are biased beliefs about the educational abilities of students of color, the subjective decision making involved in those practices, and a lack of culturally informed educational practices (Grindal et al., 2019; Togut, 2011).

As described earlier, teachers' perceptions of their students influence the way the students are treated in the educational environment. For students of color, this can lead to harmful teacher-student interactions as well as misperceptions about their academic abilities and potential disabilities. Biased beliefs include perceptions of Black, Indigenous, and Latinx students as inferior, low expectations of their academic achievement, a poor understanding of cultural norms, and a fear of Black male students (Togut, 2011). According to the bias hypothesis of disproportionality, these biased beliefs influence an important first step in the special education pipeline: the referral process (Grindal et al., 2019).

In the 2002 landmark report from the National Research Council, the panel concluded that there is sufficient research indicating racial bias in the special education referral process (Sullivan & Proctor, 2016). They specifically cited concern for the "unreliability of educational decision making in special education, noting there are many false positives and false negatives in identification" (Sullivan & Proctor, 2016, p. 280). While many teachers refer students for additional support and testing due to a concern about their abilities, unconscious bias can also play a role. Several studies have found that teachers referred students of color more frequently for special education than white students (Togut, 2011). This is a concern as an educator's negative unconscious beliefs may cause them to hyper focus on a student's weaknesses in the classroom. This hyper-focus may cause them to perceive students of color's challenges as standing out more than white students.

Lastly, the role of curriculum, school practices, and educational pedagogy have an influence on special education and the way that the academic achievement of students of color is perceived. Given the historical roots of racism, prejudice, and oppression in the US education system, it's important to consider how the current curriculum used to assess competence may not be culturally appropriate for all students. Critical race theory (CRT), a theoretical framework that examines the connection between racism, culture, and systems of power, has begun to highlight the structural racism inherent in the K-12 education system. CRT research has emphasized how the curricula in American schools perpetuate white supremacy via "Master Scripting" which is the "dominant culture's monopoly on determining the essential content of the official curriculum and subsequently the pedagogical practices used to deliver it" (Blanchett, 2006, p. 26).

The dominant curriculum used in schools systematically mutes the voices of Black Americans, preventing counter-storytelling that challenges white authority and power (Blanchett, 2006). This is done through skewing narratives of Black and Indigenous history, omissions of important BIPOC (Black, Indigenous, and people of color) historical figures from lessons, and racially disproportionate access to academically rigorous curriculum and gifted and talented programs. There have been noticeable differences found between schools that are predominantly white versus schools that are predominantly Black. Curriculum found in predominantly Black schools tend to have less emphasis on critical thinking, reasoning, and logic, which limits the opportunities available to develop these essential academic skills (Blanchett, 2006). Thus, students of color, predominantly Black students, have to struggle with racism and white privilege in curriculum as well as less rigorous content, which sets them up to be referred for special education services.

Racial Disparity in School Discipline

One of the most concerning and well-documented harmful trends in education that affect students of color is the racial disparity in school discipline and its connection to the School-to-Prison Pipeline (STPP). The STPP represents the overrepresentation of students of color, most commonly Black males, in the criminal justice system due to harsh school discipline policies (Smith, 2015). In the early 90s concerns about gun violence and drug use in schools grew, leading many US schools to create zero tolerance rules, which emphasized a harsh, inflexible approach to punishing students for "problematic behavior" such as violence, drugs, classroom disruption, and disobedience. Over time, these zero tolerance policies have proved to be destructive as they approached guiding children's behavior with intolerance and rigidity. The creation of zero tolerance policies in schools has also created a biased system that funnels students of color toward incarceration through use of overly harsh methods for mild offenses such as suspensions, expulsions, school resource officers, and juvenile courts. In an attempt to create safe schools, administrators built an environment that reinforced the harmful associations between words such as violence, bad, and trouble with Black and Brown students.

In examining trends in school discipline, it is clear that ethno-racial identity plays a significant role in the type of response a student receives. Research has highlighted how implicit bias in school discipline starts in pre-kindergarten and extends through 12th grade. While Black preschool students make up only 19% of the enrollment, they account for 47% of suspension rates in the United States (Wesley & Ellis, 2017). This high suspension rate continues as Black students are two to three times more likely to be suspended and expelled than their white classmates across elementary, middle, and high school levels (Togut, 2011; U.S. Department of Education Office of Civil Rights, 2018). Black students with disabilities are nearly four times as likely to receive multiple out of school suspensions and are three times more likely to be educated in a correctional facility (Togut, 2011; U.S. Commission on Civil Rights, 2019).

This trend is also seen for Indigenous students as they are twice as likely to receive out of school suspension (U.S. Department of Education Office of Civil Rights, 2018). While Indigenous students with disabilities account for less than one percent of the student population, they are 3.5 times more likely to receive multiple out of school suspensions and 3 times more likely to be expelled (U.S. Commission on Civil Rights, 2019). The research on school discipline on other minority groups is more variable, however, some studies have found that Latinx and Multiracial students are often punished more harshly than white students for the same offenses (Anyon et al., 2014).

These disproportionate discipline rates are very concerning as students who have been suspended or expelled have worse educational outcomes. They are more likely to repeat a grade, drop out of school, and become involved with the juvenile justice system (Anyon et al., 2014). Because these

---

Case Example: Xiomara

After Xiomara's first meeting with the school psychologist, she agreed to stop by his office and check in with him twice a week. He promised Xiomara that he was not going to force her to talk and that she could use his office to de-stress if needed. At first, she used the check-ins to sit on her phone and complain about how she hated the school. After 3 weeks, Xiomara began to open up about her previous school and how it used to be her second home. She smiled as she recalled the experiences she missed: the sound of students and teachers speaking Spanglish in the hallways, going to the bodega around the corner for lunch with her friends, and practicing with her dance team after school. Before walking to her next class, she stopped in the doorway, looked tearful, and said, "I feel like I don't belong here."

An hour later the school psychologist receives a call from the assistant principal telling him that Xiomara has just been suspended for getting into a physical altercation with another student. Students in the class reported that Xiomara suddenly started yelling and threatening another student after he touched her hair without permission.

The school psychologist has been invited to an upcoming meeting to discuss Xiomara's rise in aggressive behavior and disciplinary plan. Xiomara's parents have also been invited to this meeting.

Reflection Questions

- What do you feel would be most important to discuss during the meeting?
- How would you help the team understand Xiomara's perspective and behavior?
- How would you advocate for her?
- What plan would you recommend?

disciplinary policies disproportionally affect students of color, they are left the most vulnerable for entry into the STPP. A 2014 analysis of school discipline rates in Denver public schools found that compared to white students, Latinx and Black students had much greater odds of the police becoming involved in their disciplinary incidents (Anyon et al., 2014). They noted that referrals to law enforcement agencies depended on the ethno-racial identity of the student in trouble. Anyon and colleagues concluded that the increased police referral rate reflected the differential selection of Black and Latinx students in office referrals and the differential application of consequences by administrators (2014). This conclusion highlights the underlying mechanism that maintains the STPP: implicit ethno-racial bias.

Conclusion

While the school system is often seen as a fundamental pillar in a child's life, it's important to highlight how a child's experience in an educational environment can be shaped by their salient cultural factors. Historically, American schools have been a place where oppression, prejudice, and racism have been integrated into the experiences for many students of color. While segregation and forced assimilation are no longer dominant practices, the effects are still felt decades later. For many students of color, school is a source of hurt, shame, fear, and trauma. While progress has been made in highlighting and integrating trauma informed practices into the education system, there continues to be a lack of focus on cultural and identity-based trauma. When wondering about how to support a child who has been exposed to chronic stressors, it is important for teachers, administrators, and mental health providers to consider how a child's experience of their cultural self while at school also has an impact.

In wondering how education can shift toward developing into a culturally sensitive system, the role of school-based mental health providers becomes clear. Psychologists, social workers, counselors, and behavioral specialists can act as the agents of change for their individual schools. By adopting a wider, holistic lens that is inclusive of ethno-racial trauma, these providers can provide improved trauma-sensitive mental health screenings, services, and programming as well as provide culturally responsive consultation and guidance to staff. These changes can work to create a validating and attuned environment for students of color that promotes resilience and improves outcomes.

References

Ahram, R., Fergus, E., & Noguera, P. (2011). Addressing racial/ethnic disproportionality in special education: Case studies of suburban school districts. *Teachers College Record, 113*(10), 2233–2266.

Allen, Q. (2010). Racial microaggressions: The schooling experiences of Black middle-class males in Arizona's secondary schools. *Journal of African American Males in Education, 1*(2), 125–143.

Anyon, Y., Jenson, J.M., Altschul, I., Farrar, J., McQueen, J., Greer, E., Downing, B., & Simmons, J. (2014). The persistent effect of race and the promise of alternative to suspension in school discipline outcomes. *Children and Youth Services Review, 44*, 379–386.

Aronson, J., Fried, C.B., & Good, C. (2002). Reducing the effects of stereotype threat on African American college students by shaping theories of intelligence. *Journal of Experimental Social Psychology, 38*(2), 113–125.

Blanchett, W.J. (2006). Disproportionate representation of African American students in special education: Acknowledging the role of white privilege and racism. *Educational Researcher, 35*(6), 24–28.

Bonefeld, M., & Dickhauser, O. (2018). (Biased) grading of students' performance: Student's names, performance level, and implicit attitudes. *Frontiers in Psychology, 9*(481), 1–13.

Call-Cummings, M., & Martinez, S. (2017). "It wasn't racism; It was more misunderstanding." white teachers, Latino/a students, and racial battle fatigue. *Race, Ethnicity, and Education, 20*(4), 561–574.

Chang, D.F., & Demyan, A. (2007). Teachers' stereotypes of Asian, Black, and White students. *School Psychology Quarterly, 22*(2), 91–114.

Grindal, T., Schifter, L.A., Schwartz, G., & Hehir, T. (2019). Racial differences in special education identification and placement: Evidence across three states. *Harvard Educational Review, 89*(4), 525–553.

Huber, L.P., Johnson, R.N., & Kohli, R. (2006). Naming racism: A conceptual look at internalized racism in U.S. Schools. *Chicana/o Latina/o Law Review, 26*(1), 183–206.

Kohli, R., & Solorzano, D.G. (2012). Teachers, please learn our names!: Racial microaggressions and the k-12 classroom. *Race, Ethnicity, and Education, 15*(4), 441–462.

McKown, C., & Weinstein, R.S. (2008). Teacher expectations, classroom context, and the achievement gap. *Journal of School Psychology, 46*, 235–261.

Osborne, J. (2001). Testing stereotype threat: Does anxiety explain race and sex differences in achievement? *Contemporary Educational Psychology, 26*, 291–310.

Smith, M.L. (2015). A generation at risk: The ties between zero tolerance policies and the school-to-prison pipeline. *McNair Scholars Research Journal, 8*(1), 125–141.

Smith, W.A. (2004). Black faculty coping with racial battle fatigue: The campus racial climate in a post-civil rights era. In D. Cleveland (Ed.), *A long way to go: Conversations about race by African American faculty and graduate students* (pp. 171–190). Peter Lang.

Smith, W.A., Hung, M., & Franklin, J.D. (2011). Racial battle fatigue and the miseducation of Black men: Racial microaggressions, societal problems, and environmental stress. *The Journal of Negro Education, 80*(1), 63–82.

Solorzano, D., Ceja, M., & Yosso, T. (2000). Critical race theory, racial microaggressions, and campus racial climate: The experiences of African American college students. *The Journal of Negro Education, 69*(½), 60–73.

Sue, D.W., Capodilupo, C.M., Torino, G.C., Bucceri, J.M., Holder, A.M.B., Nadal, K.L., & Esquilin, M. (2007). Racial microaggressions in everyday life: Implications for clinical practice. *American Psychologist, 62*(4), 271–286.

Sullivan, A.L., & Proctor, S.L. (2016). The shield or the sword? Revisiting the debate on racial disproportionality in special education and implications for school psychologists. *School Psychology Forum: Research in Practice, 10*(3), 278–288.

Tenenbaum, H.R., & Ruck, M.D. (2007). Are teachers' expectations different for racial minority than for European American students? A meta-analysis. *Journal of Educational Psychology, 99*(2), 253–273.

Togut, T.D. (2011). The gestalt of the school-to-prison pipeline: The duality of overrepresentation of minorities in special education and racial disparity in school discipline on minorities. *Journal of Gender, Social Policy & the Law, 20*(1), 162–181.

U.S. Commission on Civil Rights. (2019). *Beyond suspensions: Examining school discipline policies and connections to the school-to-prison pipeline for students of color with disabilities.* U.S. Commission on Civil Rights. https://www.usccr.gov/pubs/2019/07-23-Beyond-Suspensions.pdf

U.S. Department of Education Office of Civil Rights. (2018). *2015–2016 civil rights data collection: School climate and safety [data set].* U.S. Department of Education. https://www2.ed.gov/about/offices/list/ocr/docs/school-climate-and-safety.pdf

Van den Bergh, L., Denessen, E., Hornstra, L., Voeten, M., & Holland, R.W. (2010). The implicit prejudiced attitudes of teachers: Relations to teacher expectations and the ethnic achievement gap. *American Educational Research Journal, 47*(2), 497–527.

Wang, M., & Degol, J.L. (2016). School climate: A review of the construct, measurement, and impact on student outcomes. *Educational Psychology Review, 28*, 315–352.

Wesley, L., & Ellis, A.L. (2017). Exclusionary discipline in preschool: Young Black boys' lives matter. *Journal of African American Males in Education, 8*(2), 22–29.

Adjusting Your Clinical Lens

4

Introduction

As the previous chapters have illustrated, the experiences that children have related to their ethno-racial identity have a significant impact on their behavior, emotions, relationships, and personality. If experiences are positive and meaningful, then children can develop feelings of pride, joy, and worth connected to their identity. If they have negative experiences based in fear, terror, or loss, their developmental trajectory can be altered. Instead of developing positive feelings of self and other, a child can become anxious, depressed, full of rage, or in the most severe cases, traumatized. The ripples of a negative event can be far-reaching, impacting the ease at which they navigate school, work, and relational domains.

While the impact can be significant, it is important to acknowledge that as with any type of trauma, receiving the appropriate treatment and services is crucial. Experiencing racial trauma does not put a child on an immovable downward path toward pathology. However, many children of color navigate the world without receiving treatment or services that are geared to acknowledging and naming the type of pain they have experienced. As they grow into adolescence and adulthood, they suffer in silence as they navigate through systems that lack a fundamental understanding of the type of trauma they have experienced and how to properly support them. Nevertheless, with the implementation of culturally sensitive, attuned, and responsive mental health, educational, and community supports, a child can demonstrate resilience and post-traumatic growth in the face of chronic ethno-racial stressors.

School-based mental health professionals are in the unique position of having the opportunity to implement both trauma-sensitive and culturally responsive services across several domains. Whether it is through influencing school-wide practices, shaping teacher behavior through consultation, or providing direct student support (e.g., counseling, assessment, crisis intervention, etc.), school-based mental health professionals can become agents of change who help school systems broaden their perceptual lens to become more sensitive and responsive to the experiences and needs of students of color. Working with students of color requires the adoption of a complete, holistic perspective that includes their cultural experiences. It is not enough to only examine a young person in the context of their school environment. To develop an appropriate plan of educational supports and services, educators must consider how a student's experiences at home, in the community, and in the larger society impact their ability to learn and function in the school environment.

For school-based mental health professionals, the first step in working with racial trauma and creating responsive supports and interventions is to develop a solid framework of understanding. Before intervention can occur, clinicians must first know what racial trauma is and how it can manifest in students. After creating a conceptual foundation in racial trauma, clinicians can then begin to learn how to widen their clinical lens to include issues of race, ethnicity, culture, and identity into the way they currently assess and conceptualize student functioning.

Implications for an Expanded Clinical Lens

Why is having a lens that includes identity-based trauma important when working in a school setting? As described in the previous chapter, students of color are exposed to a variety of stress-inducing experiences both in and out of school that are related to their ethno-racial identity. As children do not exist in bubbles, when these students come to school, they bring with them their history of experiences and pain, which can manifest differently in the school environment. As children and adolescents struggle to find the words to describe their emotions and experiences, it can present behaviorally. Thus, for many youth, their racial stress can appear as defiant or dysregulated classroom behavior. If a mental health professional at school does not have the correct lens for viewing this behavior and understanding the type of distress, it can lead to incorrect and inefficient conceptualization, diagnoses, and intervention.

If a student's ethno-racial distress is not understood correctly then negative dispositional attributions about their intent, personality, cognitive capacities, and future functioning can be made. For example, a Black student who is triggered by the use of the book Huckleberry Finn elopes from the classroom every day for the two weeks that the book is being read may be called defiant, disobedient, or difficult by an administrator, who may try to force the student back to class with threats of suspension. In another classroom, a teacher may wonder whether an Asian student has a learning disability after the student purposefully does poorly in class to avoid reinforcing the model minority stereotype. When thinking conceptually and diagnostically about student ethno-racial distress, it can be difficult to understand their presentation as it can "look" like many types of emotional, behavioral, and learning disorders. Behaviorally, the symptoms of racial trauma can appear as a variety of disorders including Attention-Deficit/Hyperactivity Disorder, Oppositional Defiant Disorder, Conduct Disorder, and Intermittent Explosive Disorder. The cognitive and academic impacts of this type of trauma can also overlap with symptoms of a Specific Learning Disability, Intellectual Disability, or language disorder. Lastly, the emotional aspects of racial trauma can also appear as symptoms of Generalized Anxiety Disorder, Major Depressive Disorder, Agoraphobia, Autism Spectrum Disorder, Obsessive-Compulsive Disorder, Schizophrenia, and Bipolar Disorder. While a student's presentation may include aspects of the various disorders described above, examining them in the context of a trauma reaction allows for the entirety of their presentation to be understood in a non-stigmatizing way. Rather than asking "what is wrong with you?" a racial and culturally sensitive trauma informed lens asks "what painful experiences have influenced the way you currently understand and navigate the world?"

In schools, the lens by which a student is seen through influences the type of treatment and support they receive from the system. A trauma-informed response is vastly different from one that does not acknowledge the environmental and socio-emotional influences on a student's school performance. A trauma-informed lens that is inclusive of identity-based trauma can result in more appropriate supportive services that meet all of the student's needs. For example, reflecting on the needs of traumatized students can help a school counselor to determine that an anger management counseling group may not be the most appropriate referral for BIPOC students involved in racial incidences with white peers. These implications are why becoming knowledgeable about racial trauma is so essential for mental health professionals working within the school system. In order to promote long-term success for all students, practitioners must be culturally sensitive, responsive, and trauma informed.

Racial Trauma in Schools

As described in Chapter 1, racial trauma exists on a spectrum and refers to the psychological distress and often traumatization caused by negative racial stressors including racism, discrimination, and prejudice. Common symptoms of racial trauma can include:

- Re-experiencing distressing events with flashbacks
- Increased hypervigilance
- Intrusive thoughts or images
- Intense distress at real or symbolic reminders of the trauma
- An avoidance of trauma reminders
- Exaggerated startle response
- Irritable or aggressive behavior
- Reckless or self-destructive behavior
- Difficulty concentrating
- Emotional numbness
- Emotion dysregulation
- Changes in sleeping, eating, and hygiene patterns
- Shame and/or guilt

For young children, symptoms can also include:

- Developmental regression
- Repetitive play
- Increased tantrums
- Separation anxiety
- Somatic complaints

While these may be symptoms that a child's caregivers or family members may be able to identify, sometimes a child's symptoms manifest differently when in the school environment. As children bring the weight of their home and community experiences to school, it is important to explicitly discuss how the symptoms described above may intersect with school functioning. The symptoms of a student's racial trauma can impact their cognitive and

Impact of Racial Trauma on School Functioning

Cognitive and Academic Functioning:

- Impaired ability to learn
- Lowered test grades
- Lower intrinsic motivation
- Lower confidence in academic abilities
- Poor memory
- Difficulty with reading comprehension
- Worsened handwriting
- Impaired written expression
- Difficulty concentrating on school work
- Struggles with selective and sustained attention
- Inability to manage classroom distractions
- Narrowed sense of time

Behavior in the Classroom:

- Poor attendance
- Chronic tardiness
- Increased defiance
- Lack of engagement in material
- Withdrawal from class activities
- Increase in aggression
- Increase in hyperactivity
- Changes in impulsivity
- Avoidance of school work

Socio-emotional and Relational Functioning:

- Poor relationships with peers
- Poor relationships with teachers and administrators
- Decreased self-esteem
- Changes in self-concept and identity
- Decline in emotion regulation in the classroom
- Increased anger and irritability
- High anxiety or fearfulness
- Increased sadness
- Increased sensitivity to threat
- Increased distrust of others
- Increased substance exploration

academic performance, behavior in the classroom, and their socio-emotional and relational functioning.

It is clear that the impact of racial trauma is far-reaching and can impact a student across a variety of environments. To further illustrate how these symptoms may manifest in the school environment and trigger the involvement of school-based mental health professionals, the following case examples are provided:

Case Examples

- A school psychologist working in a rural district in Montana receives an email request from a teacher to discuss a student. The math teacher is concerned about a 15-year-old Chinese American student who has recently moved to the district from San Francisco. This student's grades have steadily declined since arriving, they do not participate in class, and they demonstrate poor test performance. The teacher has tried several interventions which do not seem to be working. Recently, the student abruptly stopped speaking in class, is refusing to complete classwork, and is spending the class period with their head down listening to music. The teacher is concerned that the student may have a learning disability.
- A 10-year-old Black student is currently being discussed by the student success team due to his increasingly disruptive and aggressive classroom behavior. His teacher reports that three times a week he has episodes in the classroom where he becomes increasingly disruptive, disrespectful, and defiant which results in him being sent to the office. He has recently been suspended for the first time due to an incident where he destroyed the classroom. During these episodes, he is heard repeating strange phrases such as "there's nothing in my pockets."
- The school social worker is called in to assist in a mediation meeting between two third grade students, one who is Indigenous and one who is white. At recess they had been involved in a physical altercation on the playground, the monitor reported that the Indigenous student suddenly attacked the other student "out of nowhere." Upon interviewing the students, the social worker finds out that earlier in the day their teacher gave a lesson on "the first Thanksgiving." Prior to the altercation at recess, the students were playing a game pretending to be pilgrims.

Widening Your Lens

While understanding what racial trauma is and what it looks like is an important first step in becoming a culturally sensitive and responsive clinician, connecting this understanding to your current clinical and educational practices is essential. How does a clinician who has never heard of racial trauma begin to integrate this into their daily practices? Widening one's clinical lens requires both foundational knowledge *and* significant self-reflection. This means taking a step back to think about the way you currently gather information, conceptualize student distress, and create interventions to meet a student's needs. It also means extending that self-reflection to include critically thinking about the current systems that you exist in.

Reflection on Current Practices

When reflecting on your current practices, do you notice a tendency to operate from one theoretical perspective? How does this theoretical perspective influence what kind of information is considered important or relevant? How does this perspective impact your perception of distress and dysfunction? When gathering information about a student or a problem, how and from whom are you soliciting information? Consider how the sources of information regarding student functioning may be biased. As you gather information, what questions are you asking? Do you currently ask about a student's salient identity features? Do you assess for the presence of racially or culturally traumatic experiences? Is this something you are comfortable asking about? While additional considerations regarding the information gathering process and assessment of racial trauma will be presented in Chapter 7, it is important to consider how reflecting on your current practices is essential when working with this type of trauma.

To appropriately work with racial trauma, a clinician must have a clear understanding of what type of information is relevant and necessary for conceptualization. While gathering information about the specific behavior reported is important, it is not the entire picture. Information about the student's experiences both inside and outside the school is essential in developing a deep understanding of the student's complex distress. While it is important for clinicians to figure out an approach to information gathering and conceptualization that works *for them*, we have provided an example of the way we gather information when working with students (see Table 4.1).

Table 4.1 Information Related to Racial Trauma

Information Gathering	
Categories	*Specific Information to Gather*
School functioning	• Reason referred, student's current functioning, past functioning, and overall school experience
Relationships	• Interactions with peers and interactions with staff
Culture	• Student identity (cultural and linguistic factors), student history of traumatic experiences related to identity, and family cultural history
School factors	• Cultural and linguistic factors of school staff and overall cultural climate of the school
Contextual factors	• Current climate of their community
	• Current socio-political climate
	• Generational or historical trauma

While this chart highlights some important categories of information to assess when thinking about racial trauma, it is by no means an exhaustive list. As with any referral, gathering details about the current situation and the student's current status at school is important. It will be important to have enough information to understand how the student is currently doing, is it the same or different from how they've functioned in the past, and has their overall school experience been positive or negative. At the next level, gathering information about the student's interactions with peers and staff can highlight patterns of negative or positive relationships. Next, it will be crucial to gather detailed information about the student's cultural identity including any relevant family details. Some information to gather can include the student's salient group memberships, languages spoken, history of positive or negative experiences related to identity, beliefs, and values related to their culture, and history of any traumatic identity-related experiences in the student's family.

Next, reflecting on the current status of diversity and inclusion in the school is essential for identifying any potential triggers that exist in the school environment. Clinicians should reflect on the current cultural and linguistic make-up of the staff, any history of racially traumatic experiences between students or staff, overall climate of the school (open and accepting or segregated and tense), and the history of interracial relationships amongst students. Lastly, we encourage clinicians to place the details of the situation, the student, their identity, and the school environment into a generational, socio-political, and community context. The goal is for the clinician to reflect on how factors outside of the school may be influencing the student and their situation.

Thinking Critically about Systems

Taking a critical look at the systems that one exists in and the biases and/or limitations that may be present is also important when working with racial trauma. While issues of race, racism, and privilege are beginning to integrate into the awareness of those in power in school systems, many schools still demonstrate a lack of understanding of the unique needs of students of color. In thinking about the school that you work in, how do they currently handle conversations regarding these topics? Do they have a language or narrative that is used related to racial trauma? Does your school have a protocol or recommended services that are connected to the needs of those who are experiencing significant distress related to their cultural identity? Do school teams discuss issues related to race, identity, and trauma when discussing student progress and creating individualized plans? Is your school system set up in a way that you can observe areas of need or ask questions that could provide a more holistic conceptualization of student functioning?

Lastly, as a mental health professional you exist in a profession that utilizes a very specific classification system to articulate human distress. It is recommended that clinicians who aspire to work with racial trauma reflect on how they use the DSM, ICD, or IDEA to legitimize and label psychological suffering. While racial trauma is not in the DSM, PTSD is. Despite this, many children and adolescents are incorrectly diagnosed and can accumulate a long list of diagnostic labels as they make their way through various educational and health systems. Do you feel the PTSD diagnostic category accurately captures the experience of race-related distress and trauma? Researchers have begun to take a critical look at the DSM and how it intersects with race, identity, and trauma. Williams et al. (2018) have highlighted how the DSM's definition of trauma can be considered narrow as it does not account for the complexities of identity-related trauma. As you form your own practice in addressing racial trauma, it may be helpful for you to reflect on how diagnostic classifications help or hinder navigating this form of distress.

Conclusion

Having a trauma-informed lens when working with students of color is absolutely necessary for the accurate identification and treatment of racial trauma. For those that work in a school setting, this can be difficult as symptoms of racial trauma can vary. Unfortunately, many students who struggle with symptoms of trauma while at school are labeled as defiant or dysregu-lated and are treated without looking at the potential causes for behavior. Becoming a culturally responsive clinician requires intense self-reflection and taking a critical look at the current practices of the systems that one is a part of. As with any trauma-informed approach, working with children who have a history of stressful experiences connected to their identity requires clini-cians to ask two crucial questions: what has happened to you? How does that intersect with what is happening to you at school?

Reference

Williams, M.T., Metzger, I.W., Leins, C., & DeLapp, C. (2018). Assessing racial trauma within a DSM-5 framework: The UConn racial/ethnic stress and trauma survey. *Practice Innovations, 3*(4), 242–260.

Part Two

Clinical Application

General Guidelines for Addressing Racial Trauma

5

Introduction

As with any presenting problem, translating theory and research into culturally attuned clinical practice is essential. As described in the previous chapter,
many youth participate in therapeutic services that are not geared toward
their specific set of needs, which means they can struggle with the effects of
their trauma for years before receiving the appropriate help. As these children
suffer in silence, their symptoms worsen, their needs grow, and the impact
of their distress becomes far-reaching. The goal of this section is to apply
the conceptual information from the previous section to clinical treatment,
so that school-based mental health providers can begin to understand what
racial trauma work can look like in the classroom and therapy room. While
this specific chapter will provide general guidelines for racial trauma treatment, practical information regarding assessment, consultation, and advocacy will be discussed throughout this section.

A Trauma Informed Approach

The Substance Abuse and Mental Health Services Administration (SAMHSA)
created a framework for developing trauma-informed systems and supports
that applies well to the treatment of racial trauma and provides a helpful
structure for clinicians who are working with this type of distress for the first
time. Their framework emphasizes the three "E's" of trauma and the four

"R's" in trauma-informed care (SAMHSA, 2014). As you begin working with racial trauma in your educational and/or therapeutic settings, it is strongly recommended that you continually reflect on how your therapy interventions, group programs, and consultation services reflect a basic understanding of trauma and trauma-informed care.

Event

This refers to the circumstances of the racially traumatic event or collection of racially traumatic events (SAMHSA, 2014). This event can be a single occurrence, intermittent, or can be chronic. This event can be experienced directly, can be observed in those nearby, or can be experienced by that individual's cultural or community group.

Experience

This highlights the individual's unique and personal experience of the trauma event. It includes their understanding of the event, the meaning they assign to it, and the impact that it has had on their functioning across environments (SAMHSA, 2014). An individual's experience of the event is influenced by a variety of factors including developmental stage, the larger cultural and socio-political context of the event, and availability of relational supports.

Effect

Lastly, the short-term and long-term effects of the traumatic experience are considered (SAMHSA, 2014). The effects of the trauma can be experienced immediately after the event or can be delayed, not appearing until weeks, months, or years later. The distress can manifest physically, cognitively, emotionally, interpersonally, spiritually, educationally, and/or occupationally.

Realization

Those working to provide support for children and families who have experienced racial trauma must realize the long-lasting impact that this nuanced type of distress can have (SAMHSA, 2014). To achieve this key assumption, practitioners must have a solid conceptual foundation of issues related to race, ethnicity, identity development, bias, discrimination, and oppression.

Recognition

The individuals or systems acting in a supportive capacity must have a way to recognize or identify the signs of racial trauma (SAMHSA, 2014). This includes sensitive screening and assessment tools and procedures.

Response

The response of the individual or system must reflect an understanding of and intentional commitment to providing therapeutic support for racial trauma (SAMHSA, 2014). This is reflected across multiple levels including language used, behavior demonstrated, environment cultivated, policies created, training received/provided, and variety of supports available.

Resist Re-traumatization

A trauma-informed practitioner or system actively works to resist re-traumatizing those that it seeks to support (SAMHSA, 2014). This includes a mindful reflection on and purposeful structuring of the environment to reduce additional stressors, minimize trauma triggers, and ensure overall wellness.

Evidence-based Treatment

Although the field of psychology is beginning to shine a light on the experience of ethno-racial distress and trauma, there is still a lack of discussion on the practical aspects of trauma treatment. While there are many evidence-based treatment approaches for working with children and adolescents who have experienced trauma that are highly effective, it is important to remain reflective and curious about your approach. While these treatments are trauma informed, they were not explicitly created with this type of trauma in mind. While that does not mean they are not effective, it is important for a practitioner to consider whether the chosen approach creates a space for culture, identity, race, and ethnicity to be meaningfully discussed. It is also important to be aware of the type of population the intervention developed for. There are many approaches that are not developed specifically for children of color. As such, these interventions may lack an emphasis on cultural concepts that are important for treatment.

While remaining reflective and curious is important, having a solid foundation in a variety of evidence-based treatments for trauma is also important, as it allows the practitioner to expertly adapt the approach to meet the needs of the child they are working with. While this book will not provide a comprehensive catalog of evidence-based approaches for traumatized children, a small selection of trauma treatment approaches is provided below:

- Trauma-Focused Cognitive Behavioral Therapy (TF-CBT) (Deblinger et al., 2011)
- Attachment, Self-Regulation, and Competency (ARC) (Blaustein & Kinniburgh, 2010)
- Integrative Treatment of Complex Trauma for Adolescents (ITCT-A) (Briere & Lanktree, 2013)
- Structured Psychotherapy for Adolescents Responding to Chronic Stress (SPARCS) (DeRosa et al., 2005)

Additionally, school-based treatments have been developed to provide group intervention to the students exposed to traumatic events:

- Bounce Back (Langley et al., 2015)
- Cognitive Behavioral Intervention for Trauma in Schools (CBITS) (Jaycox et al., 2012)
- Support for Students Exposed to Trauma (SSET) (Jaycox et al., 2009)
- Trauma-Focused Coping in Schools or Multimodality Trauma Treatment (TFC or MMTT) (Amaya-Jackson et al., 2003).

Additional Clinical Considerations

While deciding what type of theoretical orientation and treatment approach you plan on using and adapting for racial trauma is significant, clinicians must also consider the importance of other clinical concepts such as: establishing safety in the therapeutic relationship, navigating transference and countertransference, identifying internalized racism, engaging in mindful self-reflection, and integrating diversity into interventions and resources. These concepts are important to racial trauma work, as they are connected to the nuanced experience of race and may come up in treatment. It is strongly recommended that before working with students of color on their racially traumatic experiences, school-based mental health professionals seek further education on how these may impact treatment and how to navigate potential hurdles.

Safety in the Therapeutic Relationship

To heal from a racially traumatic event, a child of color needs a safe and predictable environment and a strong relationship with a validating adult who provides a purposeful space for race. When starting therapy, it is crucial for the clinician to be purposeful about conveying a sense of understanding and acceptance of their experience as a young person of color. This includes acknowledging the presence of bias, oppression, discrimination, and racism in society and how it connects to the day-to-day realities of people of color. It is imperative that the clinician validate the child's experience and communicate the notion that in the therapy room they are seen, they are heard, and they are believed. In creating a space for race, practitioners must demonstrate a sense of openness, curiosity, and genuineness. Doing this will help the child see the therapist as a safe source of support; one that is capable of understanding their perspective. Depending on the child and their circumstance, it may take some time to establish safety in the relationship. However, once this happens, the child will feel comfortable bringing their difficult, confusing, and overwhelming race-related experiences into treatment, knowing that the clinician is capable of responding in a culturally sensitive way.

We want to be explicit that utilizing a colorblind approach in therapy is harmful and can further traumatize the youth in treatment. Refusing to acknowledge the realities racism and racial disparities in society is invalidating, dismissive, and promotes feelings of invisibility. Colorblindness does not foster equality or respect and perpetuates racism in the psychotherapy process. If a clinician is going to provide treatment for this type of trauma, at a fundamental level they must reject notions of colorblindness and demonstrate an openness to having difficult and at times, uncomfortable conversations in therapy.

Transference and Countertransference

Therapists must also be aware of issues of transference and countertransference, especially if there are racial differences between clinician and client.

When providing therapy, the clinician must consider the impact that their personal ethno-racial identity may have on the child they are working with. If the child has a history of traumatic experiences that have been perpetrated by members of the same ethno-racial group, then issues of transference may arise. As they talk about and process their painful experiences, feelings about the perpetrators may be projected onto the therapist. This can appear as anger, fear, avoidance, or hypervigilance directed toward the therapist during session. Clinicians must be able to recognize this, identify patterns that may be playing out in the room, and explore the transference in a way that promotes healing.

As the clinician enters the therapy room with their own history of ethno-racial experiences, it is important to acknowledge that working with racial trauma can also trigger personal feelings in the therapist. Being present in the moment can help clinicians recognize when their emotions and bodily experiences change in session. For example, suddenly shifting emotions, feelings of tension, stomach clenching, or moments of rapid breathing during a session may indicate that the client is having an impact on the clinician, which requires further reflection. It is helpful for practitioners to be aware of their own interpersonal patterns and be mindful of how they may impact the therapeutic relationship. When countertransference arises, it is recommended that the therapist engage in self-reflection on what they are reacting to, question if it connects to a part of their ethno-racial identity, allow themselves to feel the emotions triggered, and figure out if the feelings are signaling a personal need that must to be addressed.

Internalized Racism

Internalized racism occurs when a member of a racial group consciously or unconsciously maintains, participates, or supports the power and dominance of the contrasting oppressive racial group. This is done by participating in the set of attitudes, behaviors, and social structures that perpetuate the ideology that keeps them in a subordinate position. Internalized racism can be displayed through overt and explicit racist statements and behaviors or it can be covert, communicated through actions that are rooted in racist ideologies. When working with youth who have experienced traumatic identity-related events, it is necessary to assess whether their post-trauma functioning is complicated by the presence of internalized racism.

Whether it is through media exposure, family socialization, or peer interactions, children are bombarded with explicit and implicit messages about race, power, and inherent goodness and badness. As children of color grapple with their personal experiences and struggle to make sense of their reality, they may begin to internalize the negative and biased messages that are being communicated to them on a daily basis. A racially traumatic incident, regardless if it is a singular event or a collection of chronic experiences, has the power to cause intense negative feelings of hate, shame, guilt, and rage that are tied to a child's ethno-racial identity. These feelings, if left unaddressed, can result in that young person developing into an adult with an unhealthy sense of self. Thus, clinicians who provide support for children of color are encouraged to assess whether signs of internalized racism are present in the child's statements or behaviors, and if so, how that may connect to the severity of distress they are experiencing.

Self-reflection

Engaging this in this type of trauma work requires a commitment to intentional and lifelong self-reflection, both as a person and as a professional. It is impossible for clinicians to separate themselves from their history of personal experiences, beliefs, attitudes, and ideas. Therefore, one must be continually reflective of their biases and assumptions regarding race, ethnicity, identity, power, and privilege. How have your experiences shaped your worldview? Are you comfortable working with clients who are racially or ethnically different from you? Is identity something that you have familiarity talking about?

In particular, for one to provide high-quality therapeutic support, they must reflect on their own history of racial socialization, racial trauma, and areas of privilege. What comes to mind when you think of your cultural identity? Have you personally ever experienced negative race related incidents? Can you identify any areas of privilege? These types of questions allow the clinician to have a better understanding of what is happening in the therapy room and how they may be communicating meta-messages to the client. For example, a white clinician who is working with an Iranian-American teen may reflect on their session and realize that their own discomfort and guilt surrounding white privilege resulted in an awkward interaction when the teen began discussing race-related bullying.

Diversity in Interventions and Resources

Lastly, we strongly encourage practitioners to critically think about their "go-to" interventions and commonly used resources. Specifically, what do your materials, interventions, and resources communicate to the children you provide support to? It is important to consider whether these items accurately reflect the diverse makeup of the United States. For example, do the toys, books, and posters in your office depict diverse children, characters, and cultures? Do you have resources provided in other languages? When a student asks for a "skin colored" marker, what options are available? Once you reflect on the current status of diversity in your commonly used interventions and resources, it is important to then consider how you can make purposeful changes to be more inclusive and culturally sensitive.

Helpful Reminders

Without a doubt, racial trauma is a complex and painful experience that requires sensitive exploration and mindful interventions. Whether it is through therapy, consultation, advocacy, or education, sometimes figuring out how to navigate this type of trauma is difficult and many clinicians can find themselves overwhelmed with concern about how to do this work appropriately. While there is no singular "right" way to provide this type of trauma work, we do provide the following helpful reminders:

- Be mindful of the nuanced experiences of race, ethnicity, and identity
- Do not presume to know the level of distress an experience may cause a child or adolescent
- Recognize that racial injury and trauma look different for everyone
- Cultural missteps and ruptures may happen; how you repair those ruptures is extremely important
- Continue to seek consultation and additional training
- Becoming a culturally attuned and trauma informed clinician is a lifelong journey

Conclusion

Whether this is the first time you are including topics related to race and ethnicity into treatment or you have been doing this for decades, we encourage you to remain open, curious, and to practice self-compassion as you travel on this clinical journey. As you continue to learn about racial trauma and develop plans for how to intervene at both individual and systemic levels, you will likely come up against resistance. Whether it is resistance from students, parents, administrators, or the entire system, part of providing trauma work for ethno-racial stress is identifying appropriate avenues for intervention, forming realistic expectations for change, and learning how to plant seeds for future growth. Racial inequality and systemic oppression are societal issues that have formed over generations and will not change overnight. Managing your expectations for how you can help students of color is important in managing stress, reducing your risk for burnout, and making long-term change in systems. The upcoming chapters will provide additional guidance in practitioner self-reflection, managing the unique stress that comes from this type of work, and how to provide culturally sensitive and culturally responsive work from within the school system.

References

Amaya-Jackson, L., Reynolds, V., Murray, M.C., McCarthy, G., Nelson, A., Cherney, M.S., Lee, R., Foa, E., & March, J.S. (2003). Cognitive-behavioral treatment for pediatric post-traumatic stress disorder: Protocol and application in school and community settings. *Cognitive and Behavioral Practice, 10*(3), 204–213.

Blaustein, M., & Kinniburgh, K. (2010). *Treating traumatic stress in children and adolescents: How to foster resilience through attachment, self-regulation, and competency.* Guilford Press.

Briere, J., & Lanktree, C.B. (2013). *Integrative treatment of complex trauma for adolescents (ITCT-a): a guide for the treatment of multiply-traumatized youth* (2nd ed.). USC Adolescent Trauma Training Center.

Deblinger, E., Mannarino, A.P., Cohen, J.A., Runyon, M., & Steer, R. (2011). Trauma-focused cognitive behavioral therapy for children: Impact of the trauma narrative and treatment length. *Depression and Anxiety, 28*, 67–75.

DeRosa, R., Habib, M., Pelcovitz, D., Rathus, J., Sonnenklar, J., Ford, J., Sunday, S., Layne, C., Saltzman, W., Turnbull, A., Labruna, V., & Kaplan, S. (2005). *Structured psychotherapy for adolescents responding to chronic stress: A treatment guide [unpublished manual].* Department of Psychiatry, Adelphi University.

Jaycox, L.H., Kataoka, S.H., Stein, B.D., Langley, A.K., & Wong, M. (2012). Cognitive behavioral intervention for trauma in schools. *Journal of Applied School Psychology, 28*(3), 239–255.

Jaycox, L.H., Langley, A.K., Stein, B.D., Wong, M., Sharma, P., Scott, M., & Schonlau, M. (2009). Support for students exposed to trauma: A pilot study. *School Mental Health, 1*, 49–60.

Langley, A.K., Gonzalez, A., Sugar, C.A., Solis, D., & Jaycox, L. (2015). Bounce back: Effectiveness of an elementary school-based intervention for multicultural children exposed to traumatic events. *Journal of Consulting and Clinical Psychology, 83*(5), 853–865.

Substance Abuse and Mental Health Services Administration (2014, October). *SAMHSA's concept of trauma and guidance for a trauma-informed approach.* https://store.samhsa.gov/product/SAMHSA-s-Concept-of-Trauma-and-Guidance-for-a-Trauma-Informed-Approach/SMA14-4884.

Racial Trauma and   6
the Mental Health
Professional

Introduction

Addressing racial trauma, both on macro and micro levels within school systems, is as much an internalized process as it is an externalized service. Addressing this specific type of distress demands a journey that starts well before you see students, teachers, or administrators. Racial trauma can mold or rupture a child's identity in a profound way and the treatment of it mandates a complex and deep alignment on the part of the mental health professional. The internal understanding of yourself is an everchanging journey that will inform your work. This chapter hopes to highlight the intentionality one must possess outside of the school when shaping their personal and professional identity for the betterment of students of color.

Awareness

Your entrance into racial trauma work should be an intentional choice based on being informed and aware of what you might encounter. There are many things to consider and process when deciding how to cultivate your professional identity around addressing racial trauma in school systems. Navigating the racially traumatic experience of another person, especially a minor, entails quite a bit of cognitive and emotional bandwidth. Understanding the potential realities of this work will help instill or inform the creation of a sense of preparedness and readiness. You will process many dimensions of loss including safety and innocence. Negative racial encounters and the therapeutic processing of them move a child along the ERI development stages in significant and abrupt ways. With that movement will come identity-related distress as a child tries to figure out who they are and what that means to them. You will be addressing confusion and anger as students become more aware of the injustices they have been subjected to. A child's racial socialization process will impact how negative racial encounters are experienced and their comfort with discussing it. As a result, you will uncover and navigate the ripple effects of transgenerational transmission of trauma. You might also be the only or one of few mental health professionals in a school system that is addressing race-related concerns. This may result in you being flooded with students who can only turn to you for corrective emotional experiences at school.

Addressing racial trauma in school systems is not limited to working with students. Mental health professionals should be aware of what it means to challenge and restructure the racially traumatic practices of the staff, administrators, and the systemic influences that they, intentionally or not, ascribe to. This advocacy work will require you to navigate many dynamics. You will likely encounter white guilt. As you educate school staff on intent versus impact, you will have to address their cognitive dissonance and the resulting defensiveness. You will have to decide how far to push when you encounter resistance, dismissal, or devaluing of your culturally and trauma-informed efforts. You may not be permitted or allotted the resources necessary to execute certain initiatives. Understanding the dynamics that you might encounter from students, staff, and systems will help you ready yourself or seek out support to help you prepare for a sustained and impactful career.

Self-reflection

Now that you have decided that this work aligns with your desired professional identity, there is an internal processing that must occur to ensure that you do not create more racial distress for the students you work with. Self-reflection, or an increased awareness related to who you are and your positionality among those you work with and for is a continuous process that happens before, during, and after racially informed interventions. When working directly with students, there is already an inherent privilege you possess as the adult in the room. You also have an inherent privilege by not being the person in the room who is currently grappling with the negative racial encounter that prompted the therapeutic interaction. What other privileges do you possess and how might they show up in the therapeutic space?

Are you on the privileged end of differing cultural identity markers between you and the student? Identity domains including socioeconomic status, religion, gender, abilities, among others are important to think about prior to working with a student. However, racial differences are especially important to process before you start working with students who are experiencing racial trauma. You should be aware of how your actual or perceived ethno-racial identity may impact the student, their comfort, and the therapeutic process. By naming and exploring your privilege before you work with students, you are less likely to create ruptures or missteps while building rapport with the student and understanding their lived experiences.

Racial trauma work requires that you be able to discuss, navigate, and conceptualize a student's ethno-racial identity development and racial socialization. That work should start with you. You need to form an intimate and deep understanding of how your identity was created. This will allow you to understand how to guide someone else through that process and it will also increase your awareness of any views that you possess that may impact the therapeutic and advocacy process. We all have biases. You need to identify, understand, and conceptualize what biases, both implicit and explicit, are embedded in your identity. This will allow you to regulate them in a manner that does not re-traumatize the student you are working with. You cannot control something that you cannot name. You will do your students a disservice if you neglect to understand who you are and how that might interact with and impact who they are learning to be. Remember that your established identity is interacting with emerging identities. Learn to engage in difficult or uncomfortable conversations with yourself around ethno-racial topics. If you cannot do it with yourself, you cannot do it effectively with anyone else. Questions that may help your ethno-racial exploration include:

- How would you describe your ethno-racial identity?
- What has been your experience as a member of this ethno-racial identity?
- When and how did you first become aware of your ethno-racial identity?
- Was that experience positive or negative?
- What were some of the things you learned about your ethno-racial identity growing up?
- What were some things you learned about other ethno-racial identities growing up?
- How were you treated in school? How do you think your ethno-racial identity impacted your experiences?
- What are the five most memorable incidents of racism that you have experienced? How old were you for each one and how did they impact you?

- If you cannot think of any incidents of racism that you have endured, what do you attribute that to?
- Are there incidents of racism that others might recall that you caused? If so, how do you feel about that now?
- How would you describe your current race-related experiences?

Personal Impact of Racial Trauma Work

As mental health professionals, we are taught how to track and react to the distress that our clients are demonstrating. This same care and intentionality must be turned inward as you navigate the difficult task of hearing, conceptualizing, and treating the racial trauma of students and school systems. Vicarious trauma is defined as:

> a transformation in the therapist's (or trauma worker's) inner experience resulting from empathic engagement with clients' trauma material and vulnerability to the emotional and spiritual effects of vicarious trauma. These effects are cumulative and permanent, and evident in both a therapist's professional and personal life.
>
> (Pearlman & Saakvitne, 1995, p. 151)

The experience of vicarious trauma can yield clusters of symptoms and its presentation can look differently for every mental health professional. Symptoms related to exhaustion or lack of satisfaction include difficulty falling or staying asleep, frequent job changes, overworking, low motivation, and feelings of being trapped by work. Distraction or intrusion can arise in the form of feeling jumpy, dreaming of clients and their trauma, intrusive thoughts, tardiness or absences, irresponsibility, inability to be alone, poor communication, and increased work errors. One might experience misdirected emotionality in the form of aimless anger, hopelessness, blaming others, conflicts with colleagues, lack of patience, and inflexibility. Insecurity or confusion might arise in the form of worries about one's worth to clients, avoidance of trauma therapy cases, low self-esteem, and wonderings related to one's identity or worldview. Self-neglect may be present in the form of disordered eating or a sense of detachment related to one's emotions or inner self. Lastly, experiences of isolation may arise as difficulty talking about feelings, lack of pleasure, rejection of being vulnerable with or close to others, removing oneself from community efforts, and a lack of collaboration or interaction with colleagues (American Counseling Association, 2011).

These maladaptive symptoms can create externalized and internalized experiences that impact one's professional experience and range of impact. Engaging in racial trauma work can increase one's susceptibility to vicarious trauma as there are many layered and complex experiences to regulate. Holding the emotion of traumatized and confused children of color while also grappling with your own experience of racial injury or frustration with systemic happenings can be especially hard to navigate. This difficulty can arise whether there is a community trauma that you and the student have in common or if the student's personal encounter triggers your own trauma narrative. Vicarious trauma can also arise as you experience the significant distress of many students of color because you know the systemic injustices that are causing the many dimensions of loss that you have to help piece back together. The closer you get to the intense and traumatic experience of someone else, the more you will feel their pain and are impacted by it. Therefore, ironically, the more effective you are in engaging in racial trauma work with students or school systems, the more vulnerable you are to experiencing vicarious trauma. As a result, it is important to cultivate an informed and intentional relationship with self-care.

Self-care

Engagement or advocacy related to racial injustice is a powerful mission but a taxing one if done alone or often met with resistance. This is especially true when your work involves children and the systems that mold them. The hearing and treatment of race-related psychological distress without the regulation of your own internal experience can lead to vicarious trauma, racial battle fatigue, or burnout. If your goal is to have a long career where you can establish and sustain a far reach of impact and influence, self-care is a must. Before exploring personal self-care, it is important to acknowledge the professional self-care that is supervision and consultation. Consulting with other mental health professionals or seeking supervision from professionals with racial trauma therapy experience is a helpful way to get advice and additional perspective as you navigate the many presentations of this complex trauma. Consultation and supervision also help with checking for biases or missteps. Personal self-care is a more nuanced art form of cultivating a routine, practice, or perspective that will help you navigate and regulate your own internal experience of your work. Below are self-care tips adapted to racial trauma work, to help you create your own level of intentionality (Wise & Barnett, 2016).

Internalize the Service You Offer Others

Give yourself the same love, attention, care, and support that you give your clients. Approach your mental health with the same intentionality as you do that of your clients. Engage in the same racial trauma interventions that you teach your clients. Racial trauma therapy is the act of readying another human being to care for themselves and protect their sanity amid hardship and injustice. Allow yourself to adopt the same level of readiness.

Remember the Value the Work Holds for You

Redirect your focus to the drive that led you to this work originally. Process and name why this work matters to you and keep track of the successes and meaningful moments along the way. When experiencing distressful or defeating moments, holding on to your original motivation or recalling impactful moments will help.

Name the Challenges

Do not be naïve regarding the hardship you will face addressing racial trauma. You are inherently working against a steady current of engrained systemic practices and behavior rooted in white supremacy. A sense of preparedness and readiness, as much as possible, helps you to confront and navigate these obstacles for the betterment of the students you work with. Self-reflection will also help you figure out unique challenges that may present themselves during your work.

Engage in Mindfulness

Healthy sleeping, eating, and exercise habits will help you regulate your emotions and internal experience of the work. Having a health routine in addition to engaging in grounding activities will help combat symptoms of vicarious trauma, racial battle fatigue, and burnout.

Establish Support

Talk to your family and friends. While you cannot discuss the details of cases, you can name how you feel and allow them to actively help you engage in coping or restorative activities. So much of our work involves carrying the weight of others, allow those close to you to show up for you when the weight gets too heavy.

Create Boundaries

Be intentional and mindful about the racially traumatic information you digest outside of work. While auto-play features on social media and the constant presentation of racism in everyday life make this hard, be aware that since you address racial trauma in your professional work, others may look for you to hold and facilitate racial trauma experiences and discussions in your personal life. If you choose to engage, be sure to ground yourself before and after you hear about, discuss, or provide guidance around a racially traumatic event in the news, social media, or within your community. Be honest with yourself and others about when you need a break. Have times when you completely disconnect and instead engage with the parts of your world that give you joy.

Reframe Your Journey

Try not to fall into a self-critical cycle or self-deprecating journey toward your idea of perfection. Racial trauma work is like walking uphill and gathering tools and knowledge to make the walk easier as you go along as opposed to having them all before the walk began. Be kind and compassionate toward yourself as you gain the understanding, perspective, and tools to delve deeper and deeper into the art of recognizing, conceptualizing, articulating, and treating racial trauma.

Create and Keep Your Happy Spaces

Find restorative and rejuvenating activities or settings that allow you to decompress. Addressing racial trauma takes up a significant amount of your emotional and cognitive bandwidth. Explore and establish routines that allow you to recharge so that you can sustain this important work.

Be the Client

Get therapy to help navigate your own experience. Therapy will help you explore, navigate, and process race-related aspects of yourself to decrease interference with the therapeutic services you provide. Therapy is also a grounding and restorative practice that can help you regulate feelings of distress related to handling the mental health of others thus decreasing vicarious trauma, racial battle fatigue, and burnout.

Establish a Relationship with Yourself

Use self-reflection to not only understand your biases but also to attain a deep understanding of what you need to sustain a sense of connectedness and well-being. Forming an intentional relationship with yourself allows you to better show up for yourself in times of distress.

Find Your People

Seek out organizations, conferences, and workshops that will increase your clinical acumen related to racial trauma but will also provide a safe, supportive, and validating space for you to learn how to regulate your internal experience of your work. Finding a community of mental health professionals that understand who you are, what you are doing, and what you are going through will help foster a sense of belonging and decrease the tendency to isolate in times of distress.

Case Example: Tamera

Tamera is an early career school psychologist who ethno-racially identifies as African American. She is the only school psychologist of color in a school with mostly white faculty and administrators. Upon starting in this position, Tamera quickly becomes a sounding board for students to name and process microaggressions and racial injustices in the classroom. In addition to being sought out by students of color, other mental health professionals at the school refer most of the students of color to Tamera with referrals often related to conduct disorder. Seeing the need for more culturally informed practices, Tamera attempts to create seminars and workshops related to culturally and trauma-informed interactions with and between students and teachers. However, faculty attendance at these events is often low and outreach scheduling efforts are often dismissed or given low priority.

One day while walking down the hall, Mrs. Miller, an eighth-grade math teacher, asks to speak to Tamera in her office. Mrs. Miller reports that she has concerns about a new student in her class. The student is a 13-year-old Korean American female named Yu-jin who recently moved to the district. According to Mrs. Miller, Yu-jin's grades have steadily declined since she has arrived, she does not participate in class, and demonstrates poor attendance. Recently, she has abruptly stopped speaking in class, refuses to complete classwork, and spends the period with her head down listening to music. Mrs. Miller reports that she believes Yu-jin has a learning disorder.

During the first session, Tamera finds Yu-jin pleasurable and internally makes a note that Yu-jin's presentation is different than Mrs. Miller's observations. While discussing Yu-jin's performance in Mrs. Miller's class, Tamera makes the comment "I was surprised to hear that you are struggling in math." Upon making the comment, Tamera observes a surprised look wash over Yu-jin's face followed by slumping over in her chair and breaking eye contact. Immediately Tamera realizes the mistake she has made and the rupture she caused by projecting an Asian stereotype onto Yu-jin. Tamera apologizes for the mistake and processes with Yu-jin how the comment made her feel. While Yu-jin begins to engage more after Tamera's apology, the rapport at the end of the session is noticeably different from the start of the session. After reflecting on the session, Tamera realizes that Yu-jin's behavior might be due to racial distress and not learning deficiencies.

When Tamera arrives home, she is still surprised and embarrassed that she made such a culturally insensitive remark to a student. She starts to reflect on her own ethno-racial upbringing and realizes that growing up there were very few Asian students at her school or in her neighborhood and that discussions related to addressing racial injustice in her home often only included Black and Latinx communities. She also starts to recall how misunderstood or devalued she felt by teachers as the only African American student in most of her classes. She wonders if Yu-jin is having a similar experience and begins to realize that she may have dismissed Yu-jin's racial injury due to a bias surrounding the model minority trope often forced upon individuals of Asian descent.

During the next session, Tamera again apologizes to Yu-jin for the offensive microaggression that took place during the first session and asks Yu-jin if she has experienced other negative or uncomfortable racial moments at the school. Yu-jin thanks Tamera for the apology and admits that she has experienced many weird moments at the school that make her wish she had never moved here. During the course of the session, Tamera learns that most teachers mispronounce Yu-jin's name or ask if she has "an American name", she is the only Asian student in her grade, and she is often made fun of for the lunches she brings from home. As Tamera and Yu-jin start to process how these incidents elicit markedly different feelings, behaviors, and academic performances than before Yu-jin moved, Tamera's conceptualization that Yu-jin is experiencing racial distress and not a learning disorder becomes more solid as she creates a treatment plan.

Despite the progress made in advocating for Yu-jin, Tamera is still wrought with guilt over what she said and begins to engage in negative self-talk regarding her inability to recognize Yu-jin's racial injury earlier. She begins to question her ability to be an impactful school psychologist for students of color. She wonders if teachers and staff will ever allow her to effectively advocate for students of color since they have rebuffed her earlier efforts. Feeling defeated, Tamera consults with a former cohort member of hers, Brianna, as they make plans to attend a school psychology conference together. Brianna reminds Tamera that self-blaming will not help her or Yu-jin and that she should focus on continuing to repair the rupture and address the biases or blind spots that lead Tamera to not lead with the culturally informed approach that she usually does. Tamera then describes her frustrations with the school so far and her anger that Yu-jin experiences so much racial injury when Tamera is trying to implement workshops to prevent this. After hearing Tamera vent, Brianna wonders aloud if Tamera is experiencing burnout or vicarious trauma from all the racial injury she treats and tries to influence on her own. Tamera ends the call feeling hopeful about reconnecting with other school psychologists of color and learning more about self-care at the conference.

Reflection Questions

- How do you understand Tamera and her experience?
- How would you repair a race-related rupture with a student?
- Are there more self-reflection practices or questions Tamera should explore?
- What symptoms of vicarious trauma or burnout did you notice?
- What self-care tips do you think would be useful for Tamera to engage in?
- What systems of support would you seek out if you were looking for guidance?

Conclusion

Addressing racial trauma in school systems is a fulfilling yet arduous therapeutic journey with equal room for demoralizing missteps and incredible corrective experiences. Be open, honest, authentic, and curious about your students and staff as well as yourself. Name your pain so that you can name and address the pain of those you hope to serve and help. Not doing the internal work of deeply understanding your relationship with race will only be a disservice to students who are relying on you to help them understand their relationship to racial identities and encounters. The intentional and informed regulation of your internal experience and external expression will always yield a better therapeutic experience for your students and will allow you to sustain your well-being and prolong your professional impact.

References

American Counseling Association (2011, October). *Vicarious Trauma*. https://www.counseling.org/docs/trauma-disaster/fact-sheet-9—vicarious-trauma.pdf

Pearlman, L.A., & Saakvitne, K.W. (1995). Treating therapists with vicarious traumatization and secondary traumatic stress disorders. In C. R. Figley (Ed.), *Compassion fatigue: Coping with secondary traumatic stress disorders in those who treat the traumatized* (pp. 150–177). Brunner/Mazel.

Wise, E.H., & Barnett, J.E. (2016). Self-care for psychologist. In J.C. Norcross, G.R. VandenBos, & D.K. Freedheim (Eds.), *APA handbook of clinical psychology: Vol. 5. Education and profession* (pp. 209–222). American Psychological Association.

How to Assess for Racial Trauma

7

Introduction

As this book prepares you to address racial trauma in various school systems, one question still remains, how do you know that the student sitting across from you is experiencing racial trauma? As a student's ethno-racial identity intersects with the many systems that they occupy, being able to conceptualize their racial trauma is of the utmost importance for those hoping to have an impact. The journey of conceptualizing a student's nuanced experience of race-related distress holds many purposes. It allows you the ability to name the pain on behalf of the student. Alleviating the confusion that often comes from experiencing a form of distress not readily identified or addressed can increase feelings of agency and empowerment for the student. Creating a language for what the child is feeling helps deepen the compassion they have toward themselves and allows you to get closer to their experience in order to influence and propel treatment.

Modeling the naming and discussing of race-related distress also serves as a protective factor for the student as it hopefully decreases the child's susceptibility to isolation and identity denial. Assessment measures can aid the conceptualization process as well provide objective and effective methods for understanding presenting problems. They decrease the presence of bias and provide a common language to communicate to others who need to understand the student's behavior. Conceptualizing racial trauma includes many skills beyond reporting scores and teacher observations. In order to effectively deduce what a student is experiencing and how to help, you need to think of the assessment of racial trauma as a set of tools, skills, and a deep understanding of the breadth and depth of impact racial trauma creates.

While the assessment of a student of color's racial trauma experience is often initiated in reaction to a known incident of racism, whether directly or vicariously, it should also be imbedded in all initial assessment procedures after a referral has been made. When working with a student whose identity is that of an historically oppressed or marginalized group, you need to make sure that you are getting a holistic view of anything that could be impacting the behavior that prompted an encounter with you, the mental health professional.

Establishing Rapport

As with all assessment and therapeutic endeavors, establishing a sense of rapport is essential. In preparation for starting to work with a student, be mindful of how your respective stimulus values may align or misalign. Take time to think about how the child's experience of your perceived ethno-racial identity might impact their comfort level. That comfort level will impact how easy or difficult it is to establish the rapport and trust that impacts the racial trauma assessment process. Be curious and acknowledge the implications of your stimulus value, your experiences, and your biases. It is also important to have a broad idea of what rapport can look like. Traditionally cited signals of established rapport such as making eye contact are cultural constructs. Your rapport expectations may be specific to a culture that your student does not occupy. Be mindful not to reinforce racial injury by making dispositional attributions to cultural differences.

According to Bryant-Davis and Ocampo (2006), there is a three-step process of the exploration or assessment process. The first step is to focus on the therapeutic relationship. After considering the aforementioned points, it is important to find developmentally appropriate ways to bring your thoughts into the space you have created for the student. There should be opportunities created for you and the student to name your differences and similarities relative to salient identity markers. Identifying the interaction of your respective stimulus values also gives you a space to disclose your subsequent thoughts and concerns as well as help the student process their own. This moment of disclosure and discussion, models and normalizes the act of discussing race or cultural identity markers in a way that will be necessary for further assessment and treatment. In fact, in modeling a comfort with discussing ethno-racial identity, you may be already providing the student with an emotionally corrective experience. These discussions will also help you track how susceptible the therapeutic relationship is to transference and countertransference.

The second step is to focus on the therapeutic process. You want to make sure that the student is oriented to why they are with you and what your work together will entail. This includes discussing how long you will likely be working with them but most importantly, it includes making your intent well known. By clearly discussing the purpose, intention, and goals of this intervention, you are helping to create a space of safety, support, and trust. This assumes that you yourself have a grounded understanding of your purpose, intent, and goals and that they are indeed rooted in enhancing the safety and well-being of the child. While creating a safe space is important, so too is the explicit disclosure that the space is indeed a safe one. Let them know that they are welcome to discuss topics that are typically thought of as not okay to speak about (race, religion, sexual orientation, etc.). While creating and processing safety and rapport, remember that actions speak louder than words. Your actions will demonstrate to the student whether or not you are open to discussing racism or if you can hold, respect, and honor their trauma narrative. When increasing vulnerability and discussing traumatic events and subsequent feelings, the student is tracking you just as much as you are tracking them. Reacting to racial trauma narratives with dismissal, disbelief, blame, or solution-focused interventions void of empathy could traumatize the student more or negatively impact their sense of self. A safe space is one where the student feels validation, compassion, and trust in your competence. Be curious and respectful. Do not presume to know the level of distress any race-based experience may cause and do not assume that racial trauma looks the same for every student.

The last step is to focus on the trauma history. As your established rapport allows you to gather information, make sure that you get a holistic picture of the student and their psychological presentation. This holistic picture should include general history (family history, psychiatric history, medical history) as well as trauma-related data that identifies any injurious ethno-racial experiences in addition to sexual trauma, physical trauma, or exposure to war or political violence. When beginning the discussion of racial trauma exploration, it may be helpful to first introduce the idea of identity-based trauma. Discuss with the student that sometimes we have disturbing (or unfair, negative, bad, weird, uncomfortable) experiences because of how others feel about who we are. This allows for you to then ask the student if they have ever had a negative experience or been treated in an unfair way because of their race (Bryant-Davis & Ocampo, 2006). This will hopefully help you begin to intentionally screen for racial trauma or introduce the already known racist incident that has been reported as you prepare to move into the interview phase of assessment.

A Thorough Racial Trauma Interview

Once racially traumatic events (whether direct, vicarious, covert, or overt) have been identified, a culturally responsive and trauma sensitive interview is most appropriate. A thorough racial trauma interview should assess the following: the nature and timing of the incident, the relationship to the perpetrator(s) or victim(s) (if vicarious or community trauma), the subsequent actions taken or responses from others, the student's thoughts and feelings about those actions, the student's desire for other actions or responses, exposure to prior racial trauma, coping strategies, personal strengths, social history and systems of support, and family history and support (Bryant-Davis & Ocampo, 2006). It is also important to understand the cultural explanatory beliefs that the student holds in relation to the traumatic event (Dunbar, 2001). Characteristically, what is the student's behavior, affect, and conflict response and in what ways does that align or misalign with the student's response to or since the incident? Has the student experienced other traumatic events, racially centered or otherwise? What beliefs and attitudes does the student hold about their membership in their ethno-racial group and how did those come to be? What have the student's inter ethno-racial group experiences been like? What was the student's psychological presentation before and after the event (Dunbar, 2001)?

It is also important to assess the impact of the racially traumatic event or events on the student's safety. Determining the risk of further threat from the identified perpetrators or other classmates is a top priority (Dunbar, 2001). Once safety has been assessed, there needs to be a means to evaluate the student's safety moving forward and a plan to address safety concerns in the moment or in the future. Understanding the culture of the student's school is imperative when evaluating safety. Is the school perpetuating the beliefs or practices that led to the traumatic event? Will they be open to implementing action that will ensure the student's safety? Do administrators, teachers, and staff take race-related fear and trauma seriously? These questions will help determine if the school is a protective or risk factor for the student. Determining the chronicity and acuity of the events is also useful (Dunbar, 2001). Are the racial trauma symptoms or reports that the child is endorsing a result of specific traumatic events or insidious racial trauma? After assessing for safety and frequency of events, you want to identify systems of support and resources that will be helpful in protecting the student (Dunbar, 2001).

After safety has been established, you will want to assess if and how the student's nuanced experience of racial trauma has impaired their functioning. Be particularly mindful and curious about reports of intrusive thoughts, hyperarousal, numbing, intense emotional reactions, difficulty concentrating, difficulty with memory, feelings of destructiveness toward self or others, and maladaptive physical reactions (van der Kolk et al., 1996). This is explored more in-depth in other chapters, but the aforementioned trauma responses will certainly have an impact on a child's academic, social, and behavioral functioning at school. When conceptualizing the scope of impaired functioning, it is also important to note what stage the child occupies in their ethno-racial development. The developmental stage that they are in will impact how they make sense of what is happening, how their trauma is experienced, protective or risk factors, and coping mechanisms. Likewise, these negative racial encounters and how others (including you) respond will impact what attitudes and beliefs form in their current and subsequent developmental stages, thus shaping their ethno-racial identity.

Collateral information will be helpful when collecting this information as well as helpful when understanding the student's presentation from a systems approach. In the same way that you construct your interactions with the student through a trauma sensitive and culturally informed lens, do the same for their collaterals. Be mindful of how the content or method of your questioning, and your stimulus value, might impact the collateral's inclination to be forthcoming and collaborative. This is especially true when speaking with the student's guardians or family. When getting information from teachers, do not rely solely on their observations or interpretations for diagnosis. As teacher biases impact reported student behavior, you might find that one of your interventions following the assessment will be to challenge the teacher's conceptualization of the child and their behavior.

Appropriate Assessment Measures

When considering the use of assessment measures to aid in understanding a student's nuanced experience of racial trauma or determine if and how racial trauma responses relate to the referral question, be mindful of the what and how behind your choice. Each measure assesses something different or serves a different purpose and is only as good as the intention and conceptualization of the mental health professional using it. The intentional and trauma minded lens through which you pick your assessment measures must also be applied to interpreting the student's scores or responses. If from the clinical interviews or data derived from completed trauma measures, you come to realize that the student is experiencing significant racial trauma, do not compartmentalize that information.

Remember that trauma symptoms will likely impact the student's performance on standardized measures and can create a suppression of scores. Low IQ scores may not be the function of an intellectual disability but rather a function of the trauma the student is grappling with. Keep this in mind when interpreting referral requests as well. Low scores in a math class may not be a sign of a learning disability even if the teacher who requested the assessment believes it is. Also, be mindful of how trauma responses will impact the therapeutic process. If a student's racial trauma has created feelings such as distrust of authorities, avoidance, and isolation it would be understandable that they may not be forthcoming with much information during the first session and you will likely have to work harder to build rapport. In other words, make sure to apply your conceptualization to all facets of the student's interactions and do not discard the student's racial trauma responses when attempting to make sense out of seemingly unrelated data.

What should be considered when selecting the most appropriate measure to help conceptualize a student's experience of negative racial encounters? Choose a measure that aligns with the ethno-racial identity of the student (norms), age and grade of the student, the reading level of the student (can they read and interpret the text correctly or do you need to read the items and explain), the presenting concerns, what you hope to learn from the measure, and how you hope the measure will inform your treatment or advocacy related to the student. Remember that assessment measures are only as good as the clinician using them in terms of enriching a conceptualization and treatment process. Use assessment measures as one way to understand aspects of the student's ethno-racial experience, but not the only way. Placing more weight on assessment measure scores than conversations with the student, conversations with collaterals, or your observations would be doing a disservice to the student and the therapeutic process. It will also yield an incomplete picture as you will not have any context to make sense of the scores. Follow up endorsed items with questions to help you understand the context that birthed the response. Be sure to obtain information about where endorsed items occurred (if prompt was a situational) and if it occurred at school, be mindful of how the school's culture has impacted the encounter. This is especially important when ensuring the safety of the student.

As the racial trauma movement grows, so too has the selection of ethno-racial identity and/or trauma-based assessment measures that might be relevant for a mental health professional working with individuals under 18. Some examples include:

Multidimensional Model of Racial Identity Scale

This measure assesses parenting beliefs and behaviors (Lalonde et al., 2008). It would be appropriate to give to a collateral if you wanted more insight into the child's racial socialization and how that might be impacting their experience of a negative racial encounter. This measure also gives insight into the guardian's perception of ethno-racial dynamics at the school, the child's trauma history, and the child's ethno-racial identity.

Perceptions of Racism in Children and Youth

This measure assesses the experience, frequency, chronicity, attribution, emotional response, and coping response to negative racial encounters (Pachter et al., 2010). It would likely yield information that would help conceptualize the student's experiences, their beliefs regarding racism and coping, and their nuanced racial trauma presentation.

Race-Related Events Scale

This measure assesses the presence of specific types of negative racial encounters (Waelde et al., 2010). This might be useful if you have no idea if the student has experienced distressful race-related events or if those experiences are related to the student's presentation.

Ethnic Microaggressions Scale

This measure assesses for the frequency of microaggressions experienced and the student's subsequent emotional experience (Huynh, 2012).

While the acknowledgment of racial trauma as a form of distress has created some measures for children, addressing racial trauma specifically with children/adolescents is in its infancy compared to other clinical interventions or other populations. This gap increases the need for accompanying clinical interviews to be thorough. There is no one assessment measure that will tell you everything you need to know and that sentiment is especially true for racial trauma measures focused on the experiences of children. As a result of the dearth of child-focused racial trauma measures, some have adapted adult measures to fit this specific space. An example of this is the Index of Race-Related

Stress (IRRS) for Adolescents (Seaton, 2003). The original IRRS is a 46-item measure that assesses for distress in African Americans related to specific negative racial encounters. It consists of four racism subscales: cultural, institutional, individual, and collective. To adapt this measure to adolescents, ten items were removed because they were deemed to be inappropriate for that population on the basis of being advanced for adolescents (i.e., sociopolitical or historical dynamics that developmentally adolescents would not have conceptualized yet) or not being relevant (i.e., citing career-related events). When possible, language was changed to become more relevant (i.e., replacing "work" with "school"). This allowed the measure to now be accessible and relevant to minors.

While this adaptation was formal and created a new branch of an assessment measure, informal adaptation of measures can be done when working with children as a mental health professional. If there are racial trauma measures that you find helpful but they are focused on adults, try changing the language or omitting irrelevant items to better reflect the experience of the child. Additionally, if you have child-focused trauma measures that you find helpful but they do not include any items related to racial trauma, add racial trauma focused language or items to help you get the desired level of information. An example of a potential adaptation is the UConn Racial/Ethnic Stress & Trauma Survey or UnRESTS (Williams et al., 2018). This measure is a semi-structured interview that is an "aid to uncovering racial trauma, developing a culturally informed case conceptualization, and including experiences of racism in the diagnosis of PTSD when warranted" (Williams et al., 2018, p. 1). UnRESTS has the following sections: introduction to interview, racial and ethnic identity development, experiences of direct overt racism, experiences by loved ones, experiences of vicarious racism, experiences of covert racism, and racial trauma assessment (re-experiencing, avoidance, negative changes in cognition and mood, physiological arousal and reactivity, dissociative symptoms, distress and interference, duration of disturbance). While not created specifically for children or adolescents, this tool would provide structure for mental health professionals that may have inexperience or discomfort discussing racial trauma in therapeutic contexts. UnRESTS asks the client to describe racially traumatic events that have happened to them and then assesses their level of trauma based on those events. As a result, you do not have to worry about events the child cannot relate to being included. An older high school student would understand the current language of the UnRESTS and the language can be easily adapted to be appropriate for younger students. Remember that assessment measures are not the totality of an assessment or conceptualization but rather one way to gather pieces of a layered puzzle.

Informing

So, you have assessed the student and formed a conceptualization that will help inform the referral request as well as a treatment plan. How do you convey this information to others? The informing process is the culmination of your work and the therapeutic process you and the student have created. It is during this time that you will help the student and others gain a deeper understanding of the student's experience and psychological functioning. You may find yourself discussing your final conceptualization and recommendations with the student, caregivers, teachers, or administrators. Each discussion is an intervention focused on helping the student in specific ways.

When preparing for each informing moment, be mindful of who your audience is, the function of the informing, and how much the identity and stimulus value of the audience will impact how they interpret the results, recommendations, or actions items. Those prompts will hopefully help you tailor how you structure the information you present and what you include in the informing. Anticipate the ways in which your audience may need to be educated on racial trauma to leave the informing with an accurate conceptualization of the information presented and subsequent actions. Tailor your recommendations for the many systems that the child occupies. Do not only include home-based recommendations when you are aware that most of the child's racial trauma is the result of the school's culture. Be mindful, curious, and diligent about understanding how the culture of the student's school will impact the ability of your recommendations to be carried out effectively. Use consultation and advocacy to bridge any gaps between recommendations and reality that may be created by bias, power differential, or microaggressions. Remember that whatever school culture dynamics have exacerbated your student's racial trauma experience, are the same dynamics you will have to navigate to get your student the support and safety they deserve.

References

Bryant-Davis, T., & Ocampo, C. (2006). A therapeutic approach to the treatment of racist-incident-based trauma. *Journal of Emotional Abuse, 6*(4), 1–22.

Dunbar, E. (2001). Counseling practices to ameliorate the effects of discrimination and hate events: Toward a systematic approach to assessment and intervention. *The Counseling Psychologist, 29*(2), 281–307.

Huynh, V.W. (2012). Ethnic microaggressions and the depressive and somatic symptoms of Latino and Asian American adolescents. *Journal of Youth and Adolescence, 41*(7), 831–846.

Lalonde, R.N., Jones, J.M., & Stroink, M.L. (2008). Racial identity, racial attitudes, and race socialization among Black Canadian parents. *Canadian Journal of Behavioural Science, 40*(3), 129–139.

Pachter, L.M., Szalacha, L.A., Bernstein, B.A., & Coll, C.G. (2010). Perceptions of racism in children and youth (PRaCY): Properties of a self-report instrument for research on children's health and development. *Ethnicity & Health, 15*(1), 33–46.

Seaton, E.K. (2003). An examination of factor structure of the index of race-related stress among a sample of African American adolescents. *Journal of Black Psychology, 29*(3), 292–307.

van der Kolk, B., McFarlane, A., & van der Hart, O. (1996). A general approach to treatment of posttraumatic stress disorder. In B. van der Kolk, & A.C. McFarlane (Eds.), *Traumatic stress: The effects of overwhelming experience on mind, body, and society* (pp. 417–440). New York: Guilford.

Waelde, L.C., Pennington, D., Mahan, C., Mahan, R., Kabour, M., & Marquett, R. (2010). Psychometric properties of the race-related events scale. *Psychological Trauma: Theory, Research, Practice, and Policy, 2*(1), 4–11.

Williams, M.T., Metzger, I.W., Leins, C., & DeLapp, C. (2018). Assessing racial trauma within a DSM-5 framework: The UConn racial/ethnic stress & trauma survey. *Practice Innovations, 3*(4), 242–260.

Racial Trauma and Consultation

8

Introduction

Consultation is the practice of meeting with an expert for the purpose of gaining specific knowledge. As a mental health professional tasked with helping to regulate the psychological and behavioral experience of a student or students, you may find yourself tasked with being the expert in the room when it comes to addressing racial trauma in school systems. It is far better for administrators and teachers to learn from you in a professional consultation than for students of color to sacrifice their sanity and optimal identity development while school systems catch up to the need for more intentionality regarding their impact. When exploring ways to cultivate a culturally informed and anti-racist school environment, mental health professionals who understand the impact of racial trauma on children should always have a seat at the table. So, what does consultation regarding racial trauma look like? Here are some scenarios that you might encounter:

- Consulting with staff regarding the racially injurious incident(s) that is impacting a student you work with as a part of your treatment plan or assessment recommendations
- Being asked by a school to provide consultation regarding culturally informed educational practices
- Being asked by a guardian to help navigate a school-based injury or a conference with a teacher that is contributing to the child's race-based distress
- Educating a teacher on how racial trauma is relevant to their referral question regarding a student

- Challenging unjust or biased actions towards a student
- Creating anti-racist programming or racial trainings for a school on your own or at the school's request
- Helping a school navigate a community trauma or a racial trauma that had a school wide impact
- Defending the need for racial trauma or racial identity-focused groups and/or programming for students

Whether providing racial trauma-based consultation is your chosen specialty or a means to meet a treatment goal, this chapter hopes to equip you with some tools to be the expert in the room and impact change.

Administrators

There are many levels of power within school systems. Administrators are responsible for the daily functioning and overall success of a school. As a result, when exploring consultation for the betterment of student experiences, this seemed like the most appropriate starting point. When discussing the importance of prioritizing culturally informed practices school wide, it is useful to provide psychoeducation regarding the cyclical or ripple effect that negative racial encounters have on a school system. Communicating the wide range of impact racial trauma has on a school affirms the notion that anti-racist practices warrant intentional investment as racial trauma is not merely an individual or community problem that should be saved for therapy. Impacts to emphasize include increased teacher-student conflict, increased office referrals, impacted academic performance, emotionally dysregulated classrooms, and increased teacher stress.

One way to address how racial trauma is treated on a macro level in a school is to think about Positive Behavior Intervention Supports (PBIS). PBIS is "an evidence based three-tiered framework for improving and integrating all the data, systems, and practices affecting student outcomes every day" (Center on PBIS, 2019). This is a great framework to demonstrate the need for culturally responsive practices. By encouraging administrators to look at the discrepancies between desired outcomes and the data related to the experiences of students of color, you are making room for a discussion about how changes in the system can help. A sentiment of PBIS is that "because contextual fit is a core principle of PBIS, PBIS is not fully implemented until it is culturally responsive" (Leverson et al., 2019). A school's culture has the power to uplift and engage students by validating or affirming their identity, but it also has the power to invalidate and harm a student's identity with certain practices even without intent (Leverson et al., 2019). As a result, when increasing the intentionality of a school's environment, administrators must have an understanding of how their school systems have been established, how well those systems support students from varying cultures, and what changes need to be implemented to truly support and validate each student (Leverson et al., 2019). That intentionality includes holding high expectations of all students without bias or stereotyping, conceptualizing students' culture and experiences as tools to enhance learning instead of useless information to dismiss, and providing all students with equal access to effective instruction and learning resources (Leverson et al., 2019).

Leverson et al. (2019) outline five core components of a culturally responsive school: identity, voice, supportive environment, situational appropriateness, and data for equity. Identity refers to the awareness that staff and students have various significant identities that occupy the school and how those different cultures impact the daily dynamics of the classroom. Voice refers to giving space for family and community engagement. It is imperative to allow the students, families, and communities that rely on the school opportunities to express their opinions, have their perspectives acknowledged and validated, and engage in leadership around how the school system operates. Being intentional about identity and voice creates a supportive environment. A culturally responsive system is one that prioritizes a positive and reliable school culture for all. Situational appropriateness is key to creating a consistently supportive environment. Determining what behaviors will yield a supportive outcome and adapting to meet needs instead of letting stereotypes and biases drive behavior demonstrates investment in serving and supporting all students. Lastly, data for equity refers to being transparent and open to exploring and understanding the data related to how culturally responsive the school system is and intently addressing the gaps or missteps. Administrators must be committed to examining data and listening to those that experience the school with the desire to positively impact their sphere of influence for students of color (Leverson et al., 2019). All of these components will help administrators understand the impact of their school system design on students and emphasize the importance of an equitable school culture.

Creating a school culture that is equipped to address racial trauma requires change. Administrators may be more inclined to engage in technical change, or adjustments to instruction. However, as the consultant, you want to employ them to engage in adaptive change. Adaptive change is deeper as it is a change in beliefs, relationships, approaches, and mindsets which then impact policies and procedures. Adaptive change related to preventing and addressing racial trauma requires staff to be aware of how the identity of all involved intertwine and interact to the benefit or detriment of students of color. Staff must be aware of their cultural socialization and how it impacts their classrooms, meetings, and procedures. Staff are more effective when they have explored how and why they navigate the world in specific ways and are honest about their comfort level with exploring identity-based issues with students and their families. Beliefs that everyone has the same experiences or colorblindness lead to prejudiced views of what is "right" or "normal" or "appropriate." Staff should be motivated to gain a deep understanding of students' cultures and values so that students can see their identity and culture reflected in the school. It is also important to understand how the school fits into the identity of the community (Leverson et al., 2019). Whether the school is viewed as a risk or protective factor by the community is an incredibly important piece of information. Schools cannot effectively address racial trauma until culturally informed adaptive changes are embedded in every fiber of the system.

As a mental health professional addressing racial trauma, you understand that the daily humiliation of having to walk through metal detectors to enter a predominately Black school sends those students the message that society assumes they are violent. You know that walking past advanced and honors classes and seeing only white and Asian faces sends Latinx students the message that they are not smart or do not belong. There is a good chance that the administrators you are providing consultation to have not connected those dots. When discussing how to implement adaptive change, resources on restorative practices may help. A significant aspect of racial trauma is how, why, and at what frequency students of color are disproportionately disciplined compared to other students. Restorative practices address conflict while prioritizing healthy relationships and a sense of community. Harsh disciplinary approaches that exclude students (suspensions, expulsions, and referrals to alternative schools) increase the prevalence of academic difficulties, truancy, acting out, and mental health consequences (Schott Foundation for Public Education, 2014). Employing administrators to sincerely explore if their school is one in which all students feel welcome and valued, students and families engage in activities just as much as teachers, culturally inclusive behavior is demanded, and students' experiences of the school affirms their optimal identity development may help them understand why anti-racist behavior needs to be an intentional part of the school's environment.

The importance of an ethno-racially diverse staff and faculty is also worth discussing. Diversity amongst staff allows students to see their identity reflected and increases their sense of belongingness. Only being taught by white individuals sends students of color the message that people who look like them do not or cannot become teachers or administrators and effect change. Prioritizing the employment of staff of color may decrease the amount of insidious racial trauma that students face in school or may give them more outlets for support and validation when navigating racial trauma experiences. Having staff and faculty of color creates checks and balances regarding racial dynamics and allows people of color to have a hand in creating a culturally informed environment for students. However, it is not only the recruitment but also the retention of staff of color that needs to be prioritized. The school culture needs to be one in which administrators and teachers of color feel known, valued, supported, and affirmed. If the school seeking your consultation has not created an anti-racist environment for students, it is very likely that adaptive changes need to be made to be a healthy environment for staff of color as well.

Providing training resources specifically focused on racial trauma is another adaptive change that a school can make. Trainings are necessary for creating a culturally responsive environment that is able to mold to the needs of all individuals who occupy the space. Trainings create a culture and shared understanding that racially injurious treatment will not go unnoticed or unaddressed. In fact, trainings create a space in which culturally responsive and informed dynamics become the norm as negative racial encounters are consistently and fairly addressed. To be effective, trainings should include anti-racist resources for introspection, self-exploration, and ways to interact with students and fellow staff. Trainings should be continuous and reflect the idea that anti-racism is a practice and not one action done at one time. There should be structures put in place for dealing with racist behavior, how to report problematic behavior, and how to interact with students and families of color in a trauma informed way that reflects the knowledge gained from the trainings. Lastly, trainings should be proactive in that there should be a focus on how to create an environment where racial injury does not occur and also be reactive in that teachers and staff should have tools to process and/or rectify racial injury or react to community trauma.

Teachers

As we shift our consultation perspective from administrators to teachers, there is a greater emphasis on psychoeducation. As teachers spend more time interacting with students, they spend more time engaging in behavior that directly impacts the students' experience of themselves. As a result, it is imperative that teachers be invested in and educated on the importance of recognizing and addressing racist behavior as a way to decrease racial trauma. Educating teachers on what racial trauma might look like in the classroom is important. Helping teachers understand how racial trauma can be expressed is key to them interacting with students of color in a trauma informed manner. A lack of understanding leads to misdiagnosis or actions based on attributions that negate the student's lived experience. Increasing the awareness teachers have regarding racial trauma opens the window to discuss how certain classroom traditions and activities may be creating a racially traumatic experience for students. Curriculum or activities that center whiteness and negate or erase other ethno-racial cultures or their historical significance sends a message to students of color that they are not welcomed or seen. Additionally, when teachers dismiss or avoid discussing the real experience of racism and oppression in class, it sends the message that racial trauma does not deserve attention or, even worse, that the pain of people of color does not matter. If a child internalizes those negative messages, their identity will be impacted in ways that will last much longer than any lesson covered in class. Forming a more comfortable relationship and understanding of their own ethno-racial identity and stimulus value is a great starting point for teachers to honestly evaluate how culturally informed or culturally threatening their classroom is.

Providing psychoeducation regarding microaggressions is also a useful consultation task when working with teachers to address or prevent racial trauma in the classroom. Microaggressions are brief behavioral and environmental indignities that constitute messages that convey hostile, derogatory, and/or invalidating meanings to people of color (Comas-Díaz, 2016). While the term "micro" is included in this specific form of discrimination, it is important to emphasize that racial microaggressions cause significant injury and if a student encounters microaggressions on a daily basis with no corrective experience or challenge to these threats to their identity, the potential impact is devastating. Therefore, it is useful to review the impact of racial trauma on a child's identity development and be clear that moments that seem inconsequential to a teacher are greatly impactful for the student that has to endure them. It is also worth noting that while racial microaggressions are often only thought of as explicit remarks about or action towards someone's ethno-racial group membership, racial microaggressions are also engaged in around factors that are affiliated with one's race or ethnicity such as language, immigration status, or culture (Kohli, 2009).

There are three types of racial microaggressions: microassaults, microinsults, and microinvalidations (Sue et al., 2007). As a consultant it is useful to share these with teachers as they examine if their biases or classroom culture has created, supported, or condoned any of these experiences for students

Table 8.1 Types of Racial Microaggressions

Types of Microaggressions	Definitions	Classroom Examples
Microassaults	Explicit or purposeful racially derogatory behavior	1 Racial slur written on a student's locker or the bathroom walls 2 A teacher wearing blackface during a school Halloween event
Microinsults	An action or remark that demeans a person's racial heritage	1 A student's name being mispronounced with no remorse or correction from the teacher 2 Teacher accusing a student of color of plagiarism due to a belief that they could not have produced exemplary intellectual contributions
Microinvalidation	Experiences that negate the realities of students of color	1 Students being told they are too sensitive and/or overreacting when reporting being followed in stores by police 2 A student being told that their race/ethnicity did not contribute to American society or US history

(see Table 8.1). Help teachers intentionally and sincerely reflect on if the environment they have created is ever oppressive, insulting, or traumatic for students of color. If the teacher or teachers you are working with use the belief of colorblindness to direct interactions with students, be prepared to discuss how that belief system negates or erases moments for students of color to see their culture reflected as a lack of racially informed intention often defaults to white superiority or sends the message that parts of one's identity are not welcomed in this space. Also remind them that subscribing to colorblindness also means that they are not intentionally detecting or challenging the racist acts of the white students that occupy their classroom and are thus enabling an unsafe environment for students of color. If a teacher cannot think of any way that their classroom is affirming, validating, or protective for students of color, that is a telling sign that more anti-racist work needs to be done.

Consultation Considerations

When entering into consultation-based interactions with school staff around the topic of racial trauma, it is important to keep a few things in mind. The first is that the staff you work with may not be engaging in a consultation with you voluntarily. This is important to acknowledge because it may impact how you are received or treated during the consultation as well as the engagement level or motivation to change from the staff. Be clear and grounded in why you are there and be mindful of your feelings of safety and comfort. Educating others on racial trauma and asking them to identify their shortcomings as it relates to anti-racist behavior is a tall feat and likely will often be an uphill battle. Breaking down defenses or navigating the cognitive dissonance of those involved and helping them open up enough to absorb and understand the work you are advocating for is just as important and will likely be more arduous than the actual act of providing useful resources.

Finding resources that focus on how to talk about race will not only give you more information to pass on to the staff but will give you different ideas on how to start the consultation conversation. Another point to keep in mind is that some staff will not understand that their procedures, policies, or behavior are harming students of color because that was not their intent when they created them. Discussions around intent versus impact will be a significant piece of racial trauma consultation. Lastly, remember to engage in self-care before, during, and after racial trauma-based consultation so you do not burn out from racial battle fatigue. Remember that the culture that has created racial trauma symptoms for the student(s) you serve is the same culture that you will encounter when trying to better that system so please attend to yourself compassionately along the way.

Conclusion

If the idea of consultation seems daunting, it might be useful to conceptualize consultation as an extension of your treatment plans for the students of color that you serve. By thoughtfully consulting with school systems to give sound tools and psychoeducation related to the relationship between school cultures and racial trauma, you are impacting and potentially streamlining the mental health needs of the students you currently interact with and the students that will be on your caseload in the future. Consultation is advocacy and a critical aspect of being an agent of change.

References

Center on PBIS (2019). *What is PBIS?* https://www.pbis.org/pbis/getting-started.

Comas-Díaz, L. (2016). Racial trauma recovery: A race-informed therapeutic approach to racial wounds. In A. N. Alvarez, C. T. H. Liang, & H. A. Neville (Eds.), *The cost of racism for people of color: Contextualizing experiences of discrimination* (pp. 249–272). American Psychological Association.

Kohli, R. (2009). Critical race reflections: Valuing the experiences of teachers of color in teacher education. *Race Ethnicity and Education, 12*(2), 235–251.

Leverson, M., Smith, K., McIntosh, K., Rose, J., & Pinkelman, S. (2019, May). *PBIS: Cultural responsiveness field guide: Resources for trainers and coaches.* Center on PBIS. https://assets-global.website-files.com/5d3725188825e071f1670246/5d70468ef10ca28bb416e7b0_pbis%20cultural%20responsiveness%20field%20guide.pdf.

Schott Foundation for Public Education (2014, March). *Restorative practices: Fostering healthy relationships & promoting positive discipline in schools.* Schott foundation for public education. http://schottfoundation.org/sites/default/files/restorative-practices-guide.pdf.

Sue, D. W., Capodilupo, C. M., Torino, G. C., Bucceri, J. M., Holder, A. M. B., Nadal, K. L., & Esquilin, M. (2007). Racial microaggressions in everyday life: Implications for clinical practice. *American Psychologist, 62*(4), 271–286.

Advocacy in the School System

9

Introduction

Advocating for the academic, behavioral, and emotional needs of students and their families is an important part of the job for those working within the school system. The National Association of School Psychologists (NASP), American School Counselor Association (ASCA), and School Social Work Association of America (SSWAA), all identify advocacy as an integral part of the professional identity for school psychologists, school counselors, and school social workers. Whether it is advocating in a meeting for an individual student, advocating for the access to services at a school-wide level, or advocating for policy changes that would affect students across the country, those trained in student mental health are expected to demonstrate professional behavior that put the needs of students first. While advocacy is absolutely crucial to ensuring positive outcomes for a student, the role of advocate can also be a complicated and stressful experience. While needs of the student are the focus, school professionals must also work within systems, navigate hierarchies, maintain professional relationships, and push through conflict. This complicated dance between pushing for change but maintaining positive professional relationships is one that can make many professionals hesitant about pushing for radical changes.

A Broad Lens for Change

When considering how to promote the needs of students of color and those that are struggling with racial trauma, we encourage one to adopt a broad lens for what change and advocacy can look like. There is no perfect way to advocate for a student. Change can be made on a small scale (e.g., taking a biased word out of a printed school hand out, working with a teacher to pronounce a student's name correctly, etc.) or on a larger scale (e.g., implementing school-wide socio-emotional curriculum on racial trauma, removing a racist book from the district's English curriculum, etc.). It can be immediate, delayed, or a planned long-term change. It can involve a singular person (e.g., a teacher), a group (e.g., an IEP team), or can involve everyone (e.g., school-wide). Adopting a broad lens to guide advocacy means remaining open, flexible, and creative with your expectations and beliefs about implementation.

In maintaining this broad lens, one must remain reflective of the needs of the student and the desired goals. The following questions are provided as examples of reflective questions that practitioners are encouraged to ask themselves when advocating for change is required:

- What does the student need?
- What needs to happen for that student's need to be met?
- Who is involved?
- How big of a change is needed?
- Does it need to be immediate?
- What kind of change is the student expecting?
- What kind of change am I expecting?
- Do my expectations match the reality of the situation?
- Do the student's expectations match the reality of the situation?
- Has this ever been done before?
- What are potential roadblocks?
- Are there any systemic issues that would limit the type of change possible?

Advocating at the Individual Level

When working with a student with racial trauma, advocating for their needs most commonly occurs at the individual level. While providing consultation, working one on one with teachers and administrators, and addressing trauma needs in therapy are common successful advocacy strategies, we encourage clinicians to consider other avenues where they can use their position to support students and the needs of their families. School-based mental health professionals can act as agents of change and are encouraged to think creatively when reflecting on how they push for student justice.

One area where social workers, psychologists, and counselors can help is with managing parent-school conflict at team meetings (e.g., SST, 504, IEP, etc.).

For many families, school meetings are helpful and productive events, while for others they are tense and conflict-ridden as the family and school fail to see eye-to-eye. We encourage clinicians to critically reflect on the patterns within their current school and how families of color are treated by staff and how they respond to staff. It is important that clinicians be aware of and educate the other members of the team about how school meetings, 504 planning, and the special education process can be traumatizing for families of color.

Specifically, acknowledging how historical trauma and institutional racism have made the school system a historically unsafe space for ethnically, racially, and linguistically diverse students. Practitioners can help advocate for these families by reframing behaviors deemed "combative" or "distrusting" as signs that the parents' own traumatic history is becoming activated. They can also emphasize the necessity for recognizing and discussing the role that bias, power, and microaggressions can play in the process of establishing school-based supports. Reminding staff to extend a trauma-informed lens to the family can make the experience of a school meeting safer for the parents, can reduce conflict, and contribute to a positive school-home connection.

Advocating at the Systemic Level

Advocacy at the systems level for the needs of traumatized students of color is also crucial in developing more culturally attuned and responsive systems. While systems level interventions are most often time intensive with an emphasis on long-term change, advocacy at this level has the potential to help a larger number of students. It is important to emphasize that a clinician's ability to advocate and make change at the system level will be dependent on the school's resources, openness of the administrators, and the amount of time required. Not all school systems will be responsive to requests for wide scale change. It is up to the individual clinician to determine where they can be most successful.

Policy Changes

One way that school-based mental health professionals can advocate for those with racial trauma is by working with school administrators to change the harmful policies and practices that contribute to and perpetuate stressful ethno-racial experiences. As described in chapter 3, schools can harm and traumatize students of color through biased policies that are rooted in white supremacy. Specifically, clinicians can push to end the harsh and outdated disciplinary practices that systematically target Black and Brown students and contribute to the school-to-prison pipeline. By focusing on the connection between biased discipline policies, trauma, and poor mental health outcomes for students of color, they can help make the school environment a psychologically safer place.

School-based mental health practitioners can also use their education, training, and background in data-based decision making to provide culturally responsive alternatives that meet the needs of the school and the students. In providing education about racial injury and trauma, clinicians can help school administrators see how adopting a holistic and inclusive socio-emotional lens will reroute the school-to-prison pipeline. Voicing a need for the systematic evaluation of discipline data can help administrators identify patterns and areas for intervention. Additionally, emphasizing the need for a paradigm shift from punishment and control to support and development can pave the way for increased socio-emotional supports. Rather than utilizing police officers, metal detectors, and suspensions, school-based practitioners can help model a culturally responsive shift toward restorative justice, decriminalizing minor offenses, and mentoring those in need.

Additional Resources

Clinicians can also utilize their voice and professional power to advocate for additional funding and resources to provide services that meet the unique needs of those struggling with racial trauma. This type of work can be done across county, state, and national levels. Specifically, working within their professional organizations (e.g., NASP, ASCA, SSWAA, etc.) to support legislative efforts and participate in grassroot advocacy opportunities that advance the needs for increased access to comprehensive and culturally sensitive services. School-based mental health providers can also connect with the community and have discussions about the urgent needs of the students. For example, leading discussions, planning fundraisers, and applying for grants that advocate for more mental health professionals, additional training in culturally responsive educational services, and increased access to socio-emotional supports that work to reduce racial trauma in schools.

Managing Conflict

When pushing for change and advocating for the needs of a student, conflict is bound to happen. Navigating conflict within professional relationships is an important and stressful part of engaging in advocacy work. The position as a school-based mental health provider puts one in a complicated position with dual roles. At one level they work for the students and their needs, while on another level, they are an employee of the school and act as an agent of the system. They have an obligation to promote success at the student level and at the school level. This dual role means that sometimes the needs of a student may go against the needs of the school, which can lead to professional conflict.

Conflict arises when members of the school team have different views of the student, their needs, and how to support them. Historically, schools have utilized a deficit model perspective regarding student functioning, where the focus is on weakness, or problem. This negative emphasis combined with a limited lens that does not provide a holistic view of the child can result in a harsh or negative perspective toward a student struggling with racial trauma. Staff may view a child with trauma symptoms as defiant, bad, or purposeful, rather than seeing them as hurt and trying the best they can to function. This can be frustrating as a practitioner and difficult to manage as you and members of the team grapple with your contrasting views.

When managing conflict in professional relationships, it is important to reflect on your expectations for the conflict and whether they are realistic. While we may hope that others adopt our point of view, this may not be

---

Case Example: Eko

Eko is an Indonesian-American school counselor working in a private middle school, where he provides counseling support to seventh and eighth graders. Eko has been working with an Indigenous student named Kai for the last three months as he has been struggling with his family's decision to move off the reservation into the city. His transition into the city was stressful and his family has been staying with another Native family in a cramped apartment until his parents are able to find housing. Kai is grieving the loss of his friends and family that were left behind, while also struggling to adapt to a big city and the new culture of a private school with very few Indigenous students. Over the last month, Eko has noted that Kai's stress level has gradually risen as teachers have reported an increase in irritable and inattentive behavior in the classroom. Eko also notices that Kai appears on edge, is talking less during sessions, and tends to space out for minutes at a time. At grade level meetings, teachers are beginning to wonder if Kai has ADHD.

When Kai returns from winter break, he appears very dysregulated and tense. In his lunchtime session with Eko, he discloses that during the break, he was walking around the city when a group of older teens spit on him and called him racist names. When Kai returned to school, he realized that the sister of one of the teens who assaulted him, is in his history class. When he passed the girl in the hallway he was immediately overcome with fear and terrified of going to history. During the last ten minutes of the session, Kai breaks down crying, asking for Eko's help as he wants to switch into a different history class. While sobbing, Kai comments that he feels unsafe at school and wishes he could go back to the reservation.

Eko calls Kai's teacher and explains that he is dealing with an emergency and will be unable to attend his next class. For the next 20 minutes, Eko walks Kai through some relaxation exercises in an attempt to calm him down. He then takes Kai to the school's courtyard garden where they sit in the grass, discuss his fears, and brainstorm ways that Eko can help Kai feel safe and comfortable in the classroom. Eko contacts Kai's history teacher and gets a copy of the classwork that was to be completed for the day. Together, Eko and Kai create a plan for Kai to attend his afternoon classes except for history. During his history block, he will complete his work in the conference room in the counseling suite. Kai also requests that Eko let his teachers know what has been going on at home and how it is connected to what happened in school.

After school, Eko gathers Kai's teachers, the assistant principal, and the social worker at a meeting to discuss Kai's incident and develop a plan for moving forward. Eko informs the team of Kai's adjustment difficulties, grief, and assault over winter break. Eko advocates for Kai's class switch request, explaining that there are two other Indigenous students in that class, which may be more comforting for Kai. The team agrees to switch Kai into the other history class, create a check in/check out system where he meets with the social worker daily, and provide Kai's parents with a referral to a therapist in the community who specializes in working with Indigenous youth. Additionally, the teachers agreed to meet with Eko and Kai later in the week to discuss ways to incorporate aspects of his education on the reservation, into his classes now. The team agrees to reconvene in a month to evaluate how the plan is working.

Reflection Questions

- What are your thoughts on the way Eko advocated on Kai's behalf? Did he make any mistakes?
- Would you have advocated differently?
- What other supports or interventions do you believe may be helpful for Kai?
- How could you advocate for Kai at a systems level?

realistic. When encouraging colleagues to adopt a culturally inclusive lens that may be different from the way that they view situations, you may experience some pushback. During these frustrating times, it is helpful to remind oneself that everyone is on a different journey in reflecting on issues of race, ethnicity, bias, and oppression. Their resistance may stem from a place of confusion, fear, or anger. It can be helpful to make space for the other person's perspective, even if you don't agree with it. Providing this space may open up opportunities for problem solving and compromise. It is also important to emphasize that the student's physical and psychological safety are of the utmost importance and a difference in perspectives should never risk that. There is a difference between having hurtful beliefs based in hate and having a different perspective on a situation. The act of setting boundaries for yourself, students, and staff is also a powerful intervention when engaging in advocacy work.

Conclusion

As you reflect on the help that you can provide to students struggling with racial trauma, consider how advocacy factors into that picture. For some practitioners, advocacy is a strong part of their professional identity, while for others, it is a role that they are uncomfortable in. Students of color have historically been in a position of powerlessness while at school. The people in power, who are most often white, make decisions about how to educate and support them utilizing a one-size fits all approach, without considering how their experience of being ethically, racially, and linguistically different, may result in unique needs. When the complicated experience of racial trauma is added to this, students of color can become frustrated, enraged, and disappointed in the school's inability to recognize their struggle, see their perspective, and cater to their needs. This is why the role of advocate is so important for school-based mental health professionals. They can utilize their status, professional power, and role within the system to help students feel seen, heard, and cared for.

Part Three

Special Topics

Guidance for Caregivers

10

Introduction

When working with a child, you are in essence working with each experience and lesson they have absorbed before they sat down in your office. When addressing school-based racial trauma with a student, you need to be aware of all the ways in which that student has come to understand dynamics related to race, identity, and trauma. The culture of the child's home and school create their level of understanding and those two environments greatly impact each other. Family or home happenings influence what behavior manifests at school. Family settings set the stage for how children explore and advance through different ethno-racial identity development stages, which influences how they navigate race-based distress in school (James et al., 2018). To be culturally informed and culturally affirming, a school must understand the identity of the families and the community that mold the students that walk through the hall.

As a mental health professional, to understand if the school your student attends is having a positive or negative influence, you need to have a deep understanding of the experiences of the families that make up the school system. This book has focused on providing information regarding how the school impacts the ethno-racial identity of a child. With this chapter, we shed light on the impact that family systems have on ethno-racial identity development. This is important to highlight as helping a child cope with racial trauma, in any context, will inevitably involve working with the family as well. By discussing racial socialization and family system considerations we hope to provide an additional piece of the puzzle as you construct a holistic view of the child and their respective experience of racial trauma in the school system.

Racial Socialization

In a broad sense, racial socialization is the transmission of attitudes and behaviors related to world views about race and ethnicity from caregivers to children by way of subtle, overt, deliberate, and unintended mechanisms. "Caregivers" can be substituted for "important older figures" when conceptualizing how ethno-racial attitudes and beliefs are modeled for a child. This is an important note as a reminder that school staff and administrators play a role in the racial socialization of a child and as we discuss racial socialization in terms of family systems, we also encourage you to ponder what messages the students you work with are receiving from the school systems they are embedded in. Regarding family specifically, Diaquoi (2017) defines racial socialization as:

> a distinctive childbearing activity that parents engage in to prepare their children for both life in America and life as a minority in America, a means of transmitting information concerning the nature of race status as it relates to: personal and group identity, intergroup and inter individual relationships, and position in social hierarchy.
>
> (p. 515)

Racial socialization is the process by which children come to understand themselves, others, and the world and how to navigate racial encounters. In other words, racial socialization is an integral aspect of ethno-racial identity and for families of color, it is a reaction to a racialized society that historically has engaged in dehumanizing practices (James et al., 2018).

There are four racial socialization strategies that are often highlighted in research: cultural socialization, preparation for discrimination, promotion of distrust, and egalitarianism (Diaquoi, 2017). Cultural socialization is the promotion of customs, values, and traditions of one's own culture. This strategy often includes caregivers providing opportunities for children to actively engage in exploration of their ethno-racial group membership. Preparation for discrimination is the practice of promoting awareness and preparation to cope with being a member of a historically oppressed and marginalized group. This strategy often includes caregivers providing tools for how to navigate an invalidating society as a person of color.

Promotion of distrust emphasizes the idea that other ethno-racial groups are not to be trusted. This strategy often includes caregivers providing information regarding the threatening nature of others outside of the family's culture without any preparation or tools for how to respond to discrimination or how to form an affirming identity. Lastly, egalitarianism is the promotion of goals and values associated with blending in with the dominant culture, which in America, is whiteness. This strategy often includes caregivers teaching children not to see race, both their own and others, and instead focuses on cultural assimilation (Diaquoi, 2017). Anderson et al. (2018) conceptualize cultural socialization and preparation for discrimination as proactive forms of racial socialization in that the caregiver is equipping the child with protective and coping tools in preparation of negative racial encounters. They label promotion of mistrust as a reactive form of racial socialization as it usually encompasses messages that are in reaction to negative racial encounters. Egalitarianism is deemed an adaptive form of racial socialization as the emphasis is on the child modeling themselves to fit the needs and desires of the dominant culture to reduce being othered.

As mental health professionals, we are often asked to provide a professional opinion on what is healthy and what is maladaptive. When addressing the racial socialization practices of different families, it is likely that you will be asked if said practices are good or bad. While families of color are not a monolith and the function of family dynamics should be considered on a case-by-case basis, it is useful to know the research on how racial socialization impacts a child's identity and ability to navigate negative racial encounters. Individual racial socialization messages often convey significantly different messages when they are conveyed in conjunction with other racial socialization messages. If a family is only transmitting messages about race-related obstacles (preparation for bias), a child is likely to have a fatalistic outlook on life. Likewise, if promotion of mistrust is the sole strategy, the child is likely to navigate the world and their fate with an external locus of control and hypervigilant behavior. Silence about race or the realities of societal racial hierarchies (egalitarianism) leaves the child unprepared for the social injustices and stereotypes they will encounter. For children of color, color-blindness is inconsistent with the ethno-racial identity development process that relies on active awareness of race (Pauker et al., 2015). A combination approach of proactive racial socialization strategies (cultural socialization and preparation for discrimination) is most helpful in preparing and empowering children of color.

An emphasis on cultural knowledge and pride helps prepare children to interpret and cope with prejudice, discrimination, and negative group images. However, solely relying on this strategy with no preparation for bias or discrimination may increase the amount of distress and confusion a child experiences when encountering negative racial experiences. Transmitting messages that enhance racial pride and address racial barriers, in an intentional and complementary manner, instills a healthy sense of vigilance regarding racism as well as tangible evidence that those racial obstacles can be navigated. Ultimately, racial socialization should align with optimal ethno-racial identity development so there should be messages that affirm the child's identity while also equipping them with tools to protect their sense of self.

How and why families develop their style of racial socialization is also important to be aware of. When considering predictors of racial socialization, the demographic background of the caregiver and the child is worth noting. Girls are more likely to receive messages from their parents that emphasize racial pride, whereas boys are more likely to receive messages related to preparing for discrimination (Hughes & Chen, 1997). This may be because boys of color are more likely to experience overt and physically aggressive forms of racism such as police brutality while girls of color, due to the intersectionality of gender and race, often experience encounters that devalue their worth.

The age of the child also impacts racial socialization. Parents of adolescents are more likely to transmit messages associated with racial inequality than parents of younger children (Hughes & Chen, 1997). As a result, preparation for discrimination becomes a more salient form of racial socialization as children grow older. This trend makes sense if you consider identity development. As a child becomes more aware of their sense of self and the public and private regard for their ethno-racial identity, more explicit messages from caregivers related to navigating these realizations start to emerge. Also, from a safety standpoint, as a child becomes older, they become more independent and spend more time without their caregivers. Therefore, caregivers may engage in more protective forms of racial socializations as the child grows since they will not always be around to protect the child. Lastly, socioeconomic status is a demographic worth noting. Finances may impact a caregiver's and subsequently the child's, exposure or access to certain activities or places that would enhance cultural socialization.

Another predictor of racial socialization is the caregiver's own racial socialization history. Parents often recall their racial socialization experience when determining how they will raise their child. As a result, caregivers will either engage in racial socialization methods that model what they received as a child or engage in child rearing practices as a means to correct ruptures they encountered. Likewise, parental racial identity attitude is also a predictor of racial socialization processes. Parents' attitudes and beliefs regarding the significance of meaning of race in their lives and the lives of their children impacts the explicit and implicit messages conveyed. Parents who identify strongly with their racial group are more likely to communicate messages endorsing racial pride to their children and believe that racial socialization is an essential aspect of a child's success. However, parents who feel negatively about their racial status may rely heavily on promotion of distrust or egalitarianism and struggle to infuse cultural socialization or provide tools as preparation for discrimination.

Intergenerational Transmission of Racial Trauma

When conceptualizing a family system and its impact on a child's experience of racial trauma, it is also important to consider how the intergenerational transmission of racial trauma is impacting the child's presentation. Lev-Wiesel (2007) noted a bi-directional relationship between racial trauma and the family system. Racial trauma can negatively impact the family system. Alternatively, an individual's reaction to and understanding of a racially traumatic experience is influenced by their upbringing which includes the family's beliefs about ethno-racial topics and family support. How a child has been racially socialized by their caregiver can have an impact that manifests across generations. When parents transmit their ethno-racial wounds, they also transmit their trauma-related patterns of emotional intelligence and regulation. The degree to which trauma, including racial trauma, is passed on is influenced by the vulnerability and resilience of the individual (Lev-Wiesel, 2007). It is important to be aware of how cohesive and flexible your student's family is and if those levels serve as protective or risk factors when addressing racial trauma. Living with racism and absorbing the racial trauma of prior generations can result in patterns of fatalism, self-hatred, suppressed anger, resignation to injustice, and identity denial. As a mental health professional, you may be tasked with helping to break maladaptive family cycles of racial trauma responses and addressing the school's role in reinforcing those patterns may be a significant intervention.

Caregivers stuck in a cycle of racial trauma would benefit from advocacy related to the systemic practices that keep them feeling stagnant. Traumatic experiences often lead to a feeling of powerlessness as a consequence of not having been able to protect the self (Lev-Wiesel, 2007). As a result, the caregiver's sense of self in relation to the child may become damaged as they struggle to see themselves as a source of protection for the child. When assessing the racial trauma presentation of the student you are working with, be aware that there are two distinct processes of development related to the family's racial trauma dynamics. The first is the multigenerational family patterns that create the family's emotional system. It is important to assess how patterns related to emotional regulation were developed and transmitted as they will impact how racial trauma is approached. It is also important to be aware of the levels of loyalty and indebtedness within the family that keep the patterns going. The second process is the family life cycle. It will be important for you to understand how life cycle events (marriage, young children, adolescent children, launching children, leaving home, etc.) are impacted by racial trauma and how those life cycle events impact how racial trauma is addressed. Traumatic experiences in communities also play a role in the intergenerational transmission processes. It is important to be mindful of this when assessing racial trauma experienced in a family and inquire about community and vicarious trauma in addition to trauma explicitly directed at the family.

The Racial Talk Dilemma and the Education System

Intentional racial socialization is important to a child of color's ethno-racial identity development. However, families of color in America are often faced with a dilemma related to the discussion of race with their children. Ethno-racial awareness, discussion, and exploration are central to affirming identity, but America is a country with a societal norm of colorblindness. Caregivers and children experience conflict between their lived experiences and messages from society that race does not matter (Pauker et al., 2015). These colorblind norms contradict optimal ethno-racial identity development and leave the family vulnerable to maladaptive patterns of addressing racial trauma. This conflict or tension between developing one's identity or adhering to social norms is often resolved by the family either disregarding the norms and actively engaging in ethno-racial discussions (cultural socialization or preparation for discrimination) or conforming to societal norms and subscribing to colorblind practices (egalitarianism).

Schools that do not prioritize anti-racist practices exacerbate this dilemma as school culture frequently endorses or passively complies with colorblindness. Teachers and school administrators are important socialization figures for children outside of the home and whether through informal or instructional means, schools model what the child is to expect from society and are often transformative determinants of a child's identity and self-esteem (Pauker et al., 2015). A family may be engaging in intentional and effective racial socialization practices, but if the school system the child attends is doing the opposite, the work of the caregivers and the family system have the potential to be hindered or ineffective as the child grapples with which socialization process to internalize. As such, it is important that you know the culture of the school the student and family are embedded in and how that school conceptualizes and communicates race-related norms.

Role of Mental Health Professional

When engaging with a family system, either directly in the form of family therapy or indirectly in the form of encouraging family interventions to help a student, it is important to feel oriented in what you can do. Educating the caregiver on family processes related to racial trauma and helping them understand dynamics related to the child, themselves, and the family as a whole will be key. Use the information in this chapter to provide psychoeducation related to racial socialization and how this can be a tool to help treat the student's racial trauma symptoms. Encourage the use of engaging and proactive racial socialization practices and help decrease the use of avoidant or exclusively reactive strategies. While reactive racial socialization behavior will happen as traumatic incidents occur, help caregivers understand that the more they engage in proactive strategies, the more equipped and resilient the child and the family as a whole will be when direct, vicarious, or community trauma occurs.

Also emphasize the importance of the caregivers processing their own racial trauma narrative and its impact on their child rearing techniques independent of the child. This will allow the caregiver to be more intentional and aware of the racial socialization practices they bestow upon the child and will also allow the caregiver to be fully present when the child is processing their racial trauma. It is also important to remember that the patterns that have defined the family's behavior toward racial trauma will be present in the therapeutic relationship. Be aware and prepared to address how racial trauma is (or is not) named in the family, internalized racism, anger, self-blame and guilt, dimensions of loss, levels of attachment, and desensitization to the trauma symptoms of others in the family. As all mental health professionals that work with children come to know, your work is only as effective as the family's ability to enforce and affirm it. Broaden that sentiment and include school systems as well. Embrace the intertwined relationship between school and home as it relates to the child's identity development and mental health journey. To impact one is to impact the other and ultimately in order to be an effective agent of change for a student dealing with racial trauma, you need to understand all the systems that have socialized the child sitting across from you.

References

Anderson, R. E., McKenny, M., Mitchell, A., Koku, L., & Stevenson, H. C. (2018). Embracing racial stress and trauma: Preliminary feasibility and coping responses of a racial socialization intervention. *Journal of Black Psychology, 44*(1), 25–46.

Diaquoi, R. (2017). Symbols in the strange fruit seeds: What "the talk" Black parents have with their sons tells us about racism. *Harvard Educational Review, 87*(4), 512–537.

Hughes, D., & Chen, L. (1997). When and what parents tell children about race: An examination of race-related socialization among African American families. *Applied Developmental Science, 1*(4), 200–214.

James, A. G., Coard, S. I., Fine, M. A., & Rudy, D. (2018). The central roles of race and racism in reframing family systems theory: A consideration of choice and time. *Journal of Family Theory & Review, 10*(2), 419–433.

Lev-Wiesel, R. (2007). Intergenerational transmission of trauma across three generations: A preliminary study. *Qualitative Social Work, 6*(1), 75–94.

Pauker, K., Apfelbaum, E. P., & Spitzer, B. (2015). When societal norms and social identity collide: The race talk dilemma for racial minority children. *Social Psychological and Personality Science, 6*(8), 887–895.

Social Media and Racial Trauma

11

Introduction

While social media is often thought of as a means to foster a wider range of positive interactions and feelings of belongness, it can also be a tool for spreading racist behavior and adding more layers to the traumatic experience of racism. The constant feed of racial injustice and subsequent conversations or debates increases the prevalence of racial trauma and leaves individuals of color susceptible to re-experiencing racial trauma at unprecedented rates. Online racial discrimination is defined as "denigrating or excluding individuals or groups on the basis of race though the use of symbols, voice, video, images, text, and graphic representations" (Tynes, 2015, p. 2). This chapter will highlight the role social media can play in a student's experience of racial trauma.

In 2015, Tynes conducted a study to explore the presence and prevalence of online racial discrimination for adolescents of color. Students' reports included being shown racist images online, mean and rude things said to them about their race online, being excluded from online activity because of their race, and being threatened with violence online because of their race. Regarding the nature and content of online racial discrimination reports, the following themes emerged from Tynes' (2015) study: racial epithets, implicitly racist and stereotyping statements, racist jokes, symbols of hate (such as the confederate flag), threats of physical harm or death, and graphic representations or actual images of dead Black bodies. These themes describe social media practices that create dehumanizing, invalidating, and dangerous experiences for the students you will work with. Navigating race-based slurs, threats, and graphic images while using social media leaves a student of color susceptible to racial trauma responses that will inevitably impact school behavior.

Negative Online Racial Encounters

Social media can be a means of inflicting racial trauma, either explicitly or implicitly, and this dynamic has the potential to significantly impact the school culture. When conceptualizing the relationships amongst students, social media provides a way to exchange racially charged opinions and messages in a way that is not easily observed by staff. For students of color, experiencing racial trauma online from fellow classmates creates an environment in which they may not feel safe in their class. This is especially true if the school the student attends subscribes to a colorblind norm. If the student feels unsupported and unprotected by teachers and administrators when racial injury is observed firsthand, the student is much less likely to seek staff's help when trying to cope with online racial trauma.

Safety

Safety is an important dimension of loss to consider when conceptualizing the impact of social media on a child's racial trauma presentation. When a negative racial encounter occurs in person, safety concerns are often focused on the perpetrator's direct access to the student. However, social media creates a dynamic in which the perpetrator's access to the student is much wider and the amount of people who witnessed the racial injury is likely much wider as well. So, the student of color not only has to navigate racial trauma from one person but also has to navigate the response of others which can range from unsolicited advice and inquiries to aligning with the perpetrators in dangerous ways that further threaten the student's safety and identity development.

Social media's ability to embolden the sharing of thoughts that may have otherwise been filtered also impacts the ethno-racial identity of a student of color. In chapter 2, we discuss the concept of public regard as it relates to ethno-racial identity development. Imagine how a student of color's public regard is impacted if they uncover racist posts from classmates who they considered friendly peers, groupmates, or teammates. Dimensions of loss related to trust, self-esteem, privacy, control, and comfort could also cause deep identity-based ruptures.

As a mental health professional working with students, it is important to understand a school's ability to ensure safety for all students. Here are prompts to assist your exploration:

- How does the school handle racially traumatic events spread through social media, in which the perpetrator is a student or staff?

- Who would a student of color report an incident of online racial injury to at the school?
- Are in-person incidents of racial trauma addressed in a manner that would make a student of color feel comfortable discussing online racial trauma?
- What support do students of color have to name and address the impact online exposure to community trauma is having on them?
- How is safety for students of color assessed and addressed once an online racist incident occurs amongst students or between students and staff?

Exposure

It is also important to consider how social media creates vicarious forms of racial trauma that impact the child at school. Graphic images and videos of people of color being dehumanized or killed often start playing automatically on social media sites as you scroll through your feed. The constant exposure to trauma inflicted on people whose identity aligns with yours has a psychological impact. That impact is hard enough to regulate as an adult, but for children, it is even harder. Witnessing or experiencing racially traumatic events online is associated with anxiety, depression, lack of motivation, and anger (Tynes, 2015). All of the symptoms that this book has cited as racial trauma responses can manifest from constant exposure to racist events online or being the victim of online racist behavior.

When considering the impact of exposure to racial trauma endured by others, interventions targeted around supporting students who experience community trauma are useful. As a mental health professional working with students of color, you may be asked or want to create school wide spaces for students to process their feelings. Whether it be school-wide assemblies or extra-curricular spaces for students who desire specific support, there should be trauma-informed approaches for processing racial trauma on a wider scale. As students hear about or encounter negative racial encounters in their community or country, it is inevitable that discussions surrounding news footage or updates will be discussed at school or impact the behavior of students at school. Crisis interventions to support students of color that include administrators and teachers send a message to students that their school is not a place to endure while navigating racial trauma but instead can be a system of support when encountering devastating news related to our racialized society. When conceptualizing a space to address racial trauma on a school wide level, it may be helpful to consider the following:

- What is the purpose or desired intervention for this space?
- How will you determine what type of support students want or need?
- Should the space be for all students, all students of color, only students of a particular ethno-racial group, or breakout spaces for different populations?
- Is it only students that need support or also staff and families?
- How will you navigate different levels of severity related to distress and activation expressed in the space?
- What training will staff need in order to help with the space or process feelings that may come up in the classroom after the event has ended?
- Are there follow-up events or projects that the school can do with community members to help foster a relationship based on proactive engagement and not merely reactive support?

Case Examples

1   An Asian student returns home from the library after working on a group project. Upon arriving to school the next day, she is alerted by a classmate that her group mates made a TikTok video mocking her facial features and accent and that the video has spread throughout the school.

2   A few football players upload a picture of a noose to Instagram and tag a Black football player from the rival school before the homecoming game on Friday.

3   A Latinx student cries to a teacher that students have been showing her videos of immigrants in cages at the border all day. She reports that classmates have been asking if she has seen the videos, if any one there is her family, and how she feels about it.

Reflection Questions

- Have events like these ever occurred in your school or to previous clients? If so, how did administrators handle it?
- What do you believe is the best course of action for each case example?
- What kind of crisis intervention and long-term support would you give to each student?
- Do you believe support should be provided at the staff level? Why or why not?
- How would you advise administrators to handle the event on a school-wide level?

Conclusion

When addressing racial trauma in the school system, it is imperative for clinicians to understand all the ways in which students can interact with each other. Social media plays a major role in the interpersonal exchanges, both in and outside of school, that impact the ethno-racial identity development of most students. Integrate questions about social media use and social media experiences when assessing racial trauma and collecting data related to the child's culture and social practices. Be prepared to assess and address safety as it relates to the student's social media use and subsequent in-person interactions. Do not dismiss the potential impact social media has on a child's racial trauma experiences and responses. Be sure to intentionally, explore, process, and attend to the student's experience of others and themselves online as well as what increasing feelings of empowerment would look like for the student. Create a safe space for the student to explore the emotions related to enduring hateful comments from classmates or watching continuous footage of an unarmed Black man dying. You may find that you are the first person to make that space for the student.

While the students you work with are likely well versed on the breadth and depth of both positive and negative experiences on social media sites, school staff are not. Providing psychoeducation regarding the intersection between social media and racial trauma will be helpful. All of the racial trauma responses, assessments, interventions, and consultation notes covered in this book also apply to assessing, conceptualizing, and addressing online racial trauma both with students of color and the school at large. As a mental health professional, being knowledgeable about and able to validate the experience of students who have endured this specific form of race-related pain may prove to be an effective and transformative intervention.

Reference

Tynes, B. M. (2015, December). Online racial discrimination: A growing problem for adolescents. *Psychological Science Agenda, 29*(12). https://www.apa.org/science/about/psa/2015/12/online-racial-discrimination.

Racial Trauma and Police Brutality

12

Introduction

Police brutality is "a form of unwarranted physical violence perpetrated by an individual or group symbolically representing a government sanctioned, law enforcement agency as opposed to an individual perpetrator who only represents themselves" (Bryant-Davis et al., 2017, p. 853). It is the unmerited, excessive, and aggressive physical and emotional abuse law enforcement enact upon individuals (Ortiz, 2016). Compared to white victims of police brutality, Black individuals are killed by law enforcement three times as much and Latinx individuals are killed twice as much (Ortiz, 2016). Regarding unarmed victims, unarmed Black individuals have been killed by police four times as much as unarmed white people. These statistics describe a cultural landscape that is difficult and taxing to traverse as adults. For children of color who are attempting to create and protect an affirming sense of self and safety, the current social climate creates an uphill battle. The students of color you serve often have to prioritize how to survive encounters with the police over how to thrive during childhood.

Recent studies indicate that Black children are six times more likely to be killed by police than white children and Latinx children are three times more likely to be killed by police (Badolato et al., 2020). Research related to law enforcement and historically oppressed ethno-racial groups indicate that police often perceive Black children as more than four years older than they actually are. Another bias is that Black youth are often perceived as having a higher pain tolerance, which likely plays a role in the disproportionate amount of excessive force Black children endure when being reprimanded by police (Hall et al., 2016). Due to current technology and social media, we have unfiltered access to the dangerous and often fatal racial experiences of others at the hand of law enforcement. As a result, students are not only navigating experiences with police brutality in their own community but are also absorbing the experiences of others all over the country, thus increasing the prevalence and severity of racial trauma. Movements such as Black Lives Matter highlight the increasing awareness, concern, and outrage surrounding the relationship between police brutality and people of color. However, when it comes to activism, advocacy, and allyship regarding the injustice of police brutality, both the mental health field and school systems have a long way to go. This chapter hopes to increase your knowledge of this devastating form of racial trauma, the impact it has for students of color, and ways that you can be an agent of change when working with students and the schools they attend.

Impact of Police Brutality

There are many different scenarios of police brutality that people of color have endured or witnessed. However, the common denominator is the power differential. Being harassed or beaten by a government official emboldened by their sanctioned authority creates a storm of defenselessness, lack of control, and helplessness that exacerbates the traumatic nature of the encounter (Smith Lee & Robinson, 2019). The trauma exposure and subsequent trauma responses that children of color, especially those living in urban settings, endure is often compared to war veterans (Bertram & Dartt, 2008). Before conceptualizing how to address the school-based impact of this dehumanizing practice, it is important to be aware of the trauma responses associated with police brutality. Common racial trauma symptoms include: anger, nightmares, flashbacks, intrusive thoughts, anxiety, despair, avoidance, distrust, affect dysregulation, panic, self-harming behaviors, shame, difficulty focusing, shutting down, desensitization to the trauma of others, frustration, and exhaustion. All of these symptoms are worth considering and assessing when working with a child that has encountered a negative or dangerous racial experience. Experiences of police brutality or constant exposure to police brutality inflicted on others in their ethno-racial group, can additionally yield feelings of fear, victimization, hypervigilance, low self-efficacy, powerlessness, low self-esteem, and hopelessness (Sanders-Phillips, 2009).

Grief and isolation are also racial trauma responses that can be activated by police brutality. Police brutality creates a culture where children and adolescents of color have to navigate the traumatic loss of loved ones or close friends while also navigating the risk of violence or death if they encounter the police (Smith Lee & Robinson, 2019). Remember that grief can present itself in many ways and has the potential to impact meaning making, somatic symptoms, interpersonal relations, and mortality beliefs (Smith Lee & Robinson, 2019). The unfair and inhumane context of dying by police violence creates a traumatic and complex grief process for those left behind. Isolation may be a coping mechanism that a student uses to protect themselves from the emotional experience of racial trauma and police violence. Spending most of their time indoors to avoid police may be how your student navigates police violence when not at school. While this serves the function of avoiding police, it also restricts social interaction and school engagement (Smith Lee & Robinson, 2019).

This type of racial trauma certainly impacts ethno-racial identity development. Vigilance and isolation as a means of protection against police violence ruptures the exploration and commitment processes associated with cultural socialization and optimal identity development. Students of color are tasked with using their emotional and cognitive bandwidth to negotiate life in a manner that their white classmates do not. Constant exposure to police shootings or routine and aggressive police searches in their community send messages to students of color that their bodies are property and not seen as humans that deserve compassion (Jones, 2014). This can lead to feelings of shame and identity denial which is the exact opposite of what optimal identity development needs to flourish. Direct or vicarious encounters with police brutality create potentially transformative shifts in public and private regard.

There is also intergenerational transmission of racial trauma related to police. There is a long history of people of color experiencing government sanctioned violence. The Trans-Atlantic slave trade, lynching, internment, sexual assault, brutality, family separation, forced assimilation, denial of rights and resource access, and mass incarceration (Bryant-Davis et al., 2017; Smith Lee & Robinson, 2019) serve as contextual backdrops for conceptualizing the grief, distrust, and meaning making families of color hold about the police. Depression, distress, anger, suicidality, substance dependence, and internalized racism are all maladaptive patterns that can infiltrate generations within a family navigating racial trauma (Bryant-Davis et al., 2017). Police brutality also complicates racial socialization within families. Strategies that align with preparation for discrimination often include passing down protective messages such as not making sudden moves when stopped by police, speaking in a reassuring tone, and engaging in passive and submissive behavior to ensure a safe return home. However, current technology and social media have increased awareness around incidents in which those behaviors still resulted in death or injury, making it hard for caregivers to know what to say and distressing for students to decide what they will do in the moment (Bryant-Davis et al., 2017).

Advocating in the School System

Take a moment to consider how all these dimensions of impact may influence a student's relationship with their school. In addition to attempting to fulfill academic responsibilities while experiencing all the aforementioned trauma symptoms, it is also likely that these police-based trauma responses will be generalized to other forms of authority. School security or staff that represent authority for the child may become reminders of previous and current trauma and could trigger racial trauma symptoms (Smith Lee & Robinson, 2019). The mistrust and fear that is created as a result of police brutality and subsequent lack of justice, may make students of color hesitant to seek assistance from figures of authority at school.

As a mental health professional working with school-based children, it will often be your role to educate administrators and staff on the academic, psychological, behavioral, and interpersonal impacts of police brutality for students of color. Help staff understand how direct and vicarious police brutality encounters can impact a child's presentation at school and implore them to use a trauma informed lens that is rooted in relevant historical and cultural contexts. An important extension of a trauma informed practice is the creation of safe spaces. Whether you are training a school on safe spaces or you are creating them yourself in a school system, advocate for specific and supportive spaces that will allow students and staff of color to unpack their experiences with police brutality when needed at school. This will allow the student to see the school as an affirming place that is worthy of their trust and decrease the prevalence of generalized trauma.

Interventions

Conceptualizing a therapeutic journey to help students or families process racial trauma from police brutality can be daunting, but there are useful treatment methods. Due to the identity development ruptures associated with enduring police violence, narrative therapy and critical consciousness development interventions serve as effective approaches to helping students of color re-author their narratives, combat maladaptive internalized beliefs, and increase feelings of empowerment (Aymer, 2016). There is also research that supports the use of group therapy. Bryant-Davis et al. (2017) suggest that intentional and trauma informed spaces for adolescents of color are "groups that are aimed at overcoming powerlessness, marginalization, exploitation, systemic violence, and cultural imperialism through sharing their stories, learning emotional wellness skills, enhancing their relationships, and dismantling oppression by working together for social justice" (p. 863). Being able to share experiences and learn from others with similar stories in a supportive and non-judgmental space would likely prove to be cathartic and significantly impactful in combating helplessness, hopelessness, isolation, silence, and shame. With older students, it might also be useful to find racial trauma frameworks that include resistance or activism. Exploring methods of resistance as it relates to police brutality (filing complaints, attending community meetings, protesting, etc.) can redirect the experienced locus of control, increase active coping, interrupt the trauma experience, and combat internalized oppression (Bryant-Davis et al., 2017).

Remember to approach processing police violence as one piece of the racialized experience of being a student of color in America (Bryant-Davis et al., 2017). Do not pathologize emotional reactions to police violence or minimize how much the experience of police brutality can impact a student's functioning at school. Explore dimensions of loss the student may be experiencing. Also do not assume you know how police brutality is impacting the student you are working with. Be mindful of the current cultural climate and remember that racial trauma is complex trauma. Even if the referral question does not include a police-based incident, they may have still had direct, vicarious, or intergenerational experiences with police violence that is impacting their racial trauma presentation. As always, do the necessary inner work first. Explore and process your own socialization as it relates to police to ensure that you do not negatively impact the therapeutic journey the student deserves. And lastly, engage in intentional self-care when working with students' experience of police violence as it is arduous and triggering identity-based work. Attending to yourself and engaging in regulatory practices will help you prevent maladaptive transference, secondary traumatic stress, vicarious traumatization, and burnout.

References

Aymer, S. R. (2016). "I can't breathe": A case study—Helping Black men cope with race-related trauma stemming from police killing and brutality. *Journal of Human Behavior in the Social Environment, 26*(3–4), 367–376.

Badolato, G. M., Boyle, M. D., McCarter, R., Zeoli, A. M., Terrill, W., & Goyal, M. K. (2020). Racial and ethnic disparities in firearm-related pediatric deaths related to legal intervention. *Official Journal of the American Academy of Pediatrics, 146*(6). DOI: 10.1542/peds.2020-015917.

Bertram, R. M., & Dartt, J. L. (2008). Post traumatic stress disorder: A diagnosis for youth from violent, impoverished communities. *Journal of Child and Family Studies, 18*(3), 294–302.

Bryant-Davis, T., Adams, T., Alejandre, A., & Gray, A. A. (2017). The trauma lens of police violence against racial and ethnic minorities. *Journal of Social Issues, 73*(4), 852–871.

Hall, A. V., Hall, E. V., & Perry, J. L. (2016). Black and blue: Exploring racial bias and law enforcement in the killings of unarmed Black male civilians. *American Psychologist, 71*(3), 175–186.

Jones, N. (2014). "The regular routine": Proactive policing and adolescent development among young, poor Black men. *New Directions for Child and Adolescent Development, 2014*(143), 33–54.

Ortiz, M. A. (2016). "Stop resisting!": An exploratory study of police brutality and its impacts on Black and Latino males, their communities, mental health and healing. [Master's Thesis, Smith College]. Theses, Dissertations, and Projects.

Sanders-Phillips, K. (2009). Racial discrimination: A continuum of violence exposure for children of color. *Clinical Child and Family Psychology Review, 12*(2), 174–195.

Smith Lee, J. R., & Robinson, M. (2019). "That's my number one fear in life. It's the police": Examining young Black men's exposures to trauma and loss resulting from police violence and police killings. *Journal of Black Psychology, 45*(3), 143–184.

Racial Trauma in Immigrant and Refugee Families

13

Case Example

Aapti is a six-year-old who just came off the plane with her grandparents from India, as they are in the process of moving to the United States. Aapti's parents have been living in Nebraska for six months, waiting until they saved up enough money to send for her. Looking around the airport, Aapti is overwhelmed with how different the people look, speak, and dress. On the way home, Aapti's family stops at a gas station. As she looks out the window, she notices a man walk by her father and call him a strange word. She does not know what it means, but she sees how it makes her father upset. She notices her father and this man exchange some more words before her father gets back in the car and aggressively drives off. Her father looks angry and her mother looks scared. Aapti is confused about what is happening and asks the adults in the car what the strange word meant. No one answers her question. Quietly, she returns to looking out the window and after five minutes she begins to feel her stomach ache.

Introduction

For many, the emotional experience of moving to a new country is multifaceted and complex. On one hand, it is exciting as they are filled with feelings of hope about their future in a new place. On the other hand, the experience of moving to a new country is terrifying, as they leave the familiar behind and embark on a journey to a foreign land with different customs, languages, and societal practices. For some, the choice to leave their home is not voluntary and is forced upon them due to issues with safety in their home country. One's experience in a new country is also complicated by the psychosocial, economical, and socio-political challenges that come from being identified as an immigrant, refugee, or asylum seeker. Issues such as finding work, struggling with low wages, a lack of access to resources, and fear of being forced out of the country contribute to negative health and wellness outcomes for this population (Gonzales et al., 2013; Jaycox et al., 2002).

In the United States, the experience of immigrants, refugees, and asylum seekers is further impacted by the intersection of xenophobia and racism. Immigrants can be understood as those who make a conscious decision to leave their country of origin with the purpose of resettling in a new country. By contrast, refugees are forced to leave their country of origin because their safety is compromised. Conditions that prompt a forced move can include war, violence, and persecution. An asylum seeker is a related term and represents a person who is seeking international protection from another country, but their refugee status has not yet been determined (Segal & Mayadas, 2005). The experience of immigration can be traumatic in itself and the pain of this experience can be exacerbated if the person is exposed to discriminatory or oppressive acts that are connected to their cultural identity (Gonzales et al., 2013). This means that in addition to carrying the weight of their pre-migration trauma, they also have to navigate life in a new country while experiencing post-migration trauma. This distress is amplified by today's hostile anti-immigrant political climate that has created a rise in fear and anxiety in immigrant communities (Gonzales et al., 2013).

Understanding the experiences of immigrant and refugee families is essential for school-based mental health professionals as the number of children in US schools who are foreign-born increases each year. Due to a lack of access to community resources, immigrant and refugee students are statistically less likely to receive the necessary mental health supports than their peers (Gonzales et al., 2013). For some, schools are the only avenue where support can be received. This illustrates the important role that school-based providers can have in meeting the needs of this unique population.

Challenges Experienced by Immigrant and Refugee Families

Families who leave their homeland to live in a new country experience significant adjustment-related stress as they adapt to their new life circumstances.

The term immigrant trauma is used to describe the complex psychological, social, and cultural stressors that are unique to the immigration process (Perez Foster, 2001). When settling in the US, families can struggle with the abrupt removal of social networks contributing to feelings of loneliness and isolation. Additionally, the contrast between the hopes they had for financial success vs the reality of changes in socio-economic status can contribute to feelings of disappointment and sadness (Perez Foster, 2001). Mental health research has begun to recognize that while the experience of this stress tends to be typical for this population, the cumulative effect of the stress can lead to clinical problems. For many families, this adjustment-related stress is short-lived and stabilizes after they establish a new sense of normalcy. However, there are some families who remain stressed for much longer periods of time. This adjustment stress combined with traumatic experiences before, during, and after the migration process can lead to PTSD, clinical anxiety, and clinical depression (Gonzales et al., 2013; Jaycox et al., 2002; Perez Foster, 2001).

For refugee families and some immigrant families, chronic trauma in their country of origin is what triggered the move. These traumatic experiences, also known as pre-migration trauma, are often ignored or avoided after the move as a way of coping with more urgent triggers of stress (e.g., language acquisition, housing, employment, school, etc.). As described above, these experiences can include war, community violence, gang violence, threat of persecution, and sexual violence. Trauma experienced during migration refers to the stressful experiences that the family went through to relocate. For those that are undocumented, the need to evade law enforcement often increases their risk for this type of trauma. For example, women traveling from Central America alone may seek the services of "coyotes" (illegal travel brokers), which may subject them to a variety of traumatic experiences including sexual assault, forced labor, and physical abuse (Perez Foster, 2001). Other traumatic experiences that many undocumented individuals experience in their quest to reach the US include: witnessing drownings, confinement in small shipping containers or small living quarters, physical injuries from travel, and extreme physical exhaustion. Lastly, trauma experienced once the family has settled in the new country is called post-migration trauma. This type of trauma includes experiences in temporary resettlement areas / camps, detention centers, and in their permanent post-migration community (Perez Foster, 2001).

Unfortunately, research has demonstrated how trauma experienced during migration and post-migration can exacerbate the impact of stress and trauma experienced pre-migration (Perez Foster, 2001). This means, the path an individual takes in their resettlement journey is extremely important and has the potential to significantly impact future functioning. This path is even more important for children as they do not have the cognitive capacity to fully understand the stressful experiences and look to their parents for understanding. Studies on immigrant and refugee children have found that post-migration, they demonstrate much higher rates of PTSD than non-immigrant children (Jaycox et al., 2002). Unfortunately, for immigrant and refugee children of color, their experiences of racism, discrimination, and xenophobia can add to the cumulative trauma they are already carrying, leading to a worsening of symptoms and a complex presentation. New research has identified the impact that institutional, systemic, and cultural practices and biases can have on this population's mental health outcomes (Kim, 2016). Specifically, the ethno-racial background of the individual, their experiences of discrimination, and their neighborhood environments can make them more at risk for worse outcomes. Therefore, not only are these children struggling with the feelings about their previous experiences but now have to navigate the stressful experiences related to multiple parts of their cultural identity at the same time.

Intersectionality and Racial Trauma

Given the current socio-political climate of the US, immigrant and refugee children of color experience marginalization due to multiple aspects of their cultural identity. Country of origin, ethno-racial identity, language(s) spoken, and religious identity all intersect to create a unique cross-section of discrimination and privilege. These various identities intersect in ways that impact how they are viewed, understood, and treated in the US. Within the last decade, debates about immigration, immigration policies, human rights, and social justice have become more purposeful topics of conversation amongst families, schools, communities, and in politics. With the rise in social media usage and 24/7 news stations, immigrant and refugee families have become exposed to chronic hurtful, invalidating, and prejudiced beliefs connected to their identity. Additionally, for those that are undocumented, a rise in policing and deportation practices have left families in a constant state of fear. Children in undocumented families are seeing videos about ICE raids, learning about deplorable conditions in detention centers, and are worried whether their families are going to be separated without notice. Throughout all of this, immigrant and refugee children are witnessing the community-level trauma occurring around them and are trying to make sense of it.

This cumulative identity-based trauma can have a significant impact on a child's identity development and functioning across environments. As children grow and begin to figure out who they are and how they see themselves, prolonged exposure to this complex form of racial trauma can result in negative feelings about their immigration status, internalized xenophobia, and internalized racism. This type of trauma can also impact a child's acculturation process once they've settled in the US. After moving to a new country, children must figure out the balance between keeping features of their culture of origin and adopting features of their host country (Gonzales et al., 2013; Perez Foster, 2001). Chronic traumatic experiences related to one's identity can skew this process and result in a rigid approach. Rather than striking a balance, the child may completely reject either their culture of origin or the culture of the US. Language acquisition can also be impacted by this maladaptive and rigid acculturation strategy. Children may refuse to speak their primary language in favor of English or may choose to push back against their English education.

Areas for Intervention

Given the significant impact that this complex racial trauma can have on immigrant and refugee children, school-based mental health professionals must be prepared to address it in the school environment. Unfortunately, these traumatic intersectional experiences are not restricted to one environment and also occur in school for many children. Instead of school being a place of safety for these students, it becomes another avenue to experience hurt and feel unwelcome. We argue that school-based clinicians can have an important role in creating culturally responsive supports and interventions for these students to reduce feelings of distress and promote healthy identity development. Specifically, clinicians can use their skills of consulting, advocating, and counseling to meet the needs of immigrant and refugee students.

School-based practitioners can help their schools become more aware of the unique experiences and needs of these types of students. First, practitioners are encouraged to reflect on the specific needs of their school to determine the best course of action. At the individual student level, clinicians are encouraged to consider how a student's migration trauma may be influencing their learning challenges, adapt more holistic and culturally informed conceptualizations of a student's distress, and invite issues related to their immigration experience into the therapy room. At the staff level, clinicians can provide in-service workshops on meeting the educational needs of

Case Example: Oscar

Oscar is a 14-year-old boy who was born in Guatemala but is currently living with his parents in New York. Oscar and his parents moved to the United States when he was four years old, as they were trying to get away from the gang violence in their home community. They arrived in the US, acquired green cards, and moved around until they found a permanent home in a refugee resettlement area. Oscar's parents were engineers and worked hard to provide financially so that they could achieve the American dream.

Shortly after Oscar's 13th birthday, his father lost his job and his family had to downsize to a smaller home. A couple of months later, his mother also lost her job and the family began to experience significant financial struggles. As they downsized again, into a two-bedroom apartment, Oscar became anxious as he worried about whether his family could afford to stay in the US. Eventually, his mother was able to find another job; however, it was four hours away. His parents made the decision that Oscar and his father would remain in their apartment, while during the week Oscar's mother would live near her job and would return home every weekend. Although Oscar was superficially supportive, he fell into a depression as the stress of the family's financial troubles and the family separation became too high.

Six months later, Oscar was now 14 and struggling with anxiety, sadness, conflictual parent-child interactions, and passive suicidal ideation. His parents were frustrated as they felt he was pushing them away and locking himself in his room. During this time, Oscar's grades fell and he began refusing to go to school. He told his parents that school was too stressful, made him anxious, and would cry when they forced him to attend. The parents reached out to the school counselor for help with his school refusal. The school counselor met with Oscar, helped create a tiered attendance plan, and set a schedule for morning check-ins with the school psychologist upon arriving at school. The counselor also agreed to start meeting with Oscar for counseling twice a week as his parents struggled to find an affordable outpatient therapist.

During his initial sessions, Oscar disclosed that he did not want to attend school because his peers were saying upsetting things to him at lunch. He explained that because he was in the honors classes, the majority of his peer group was made up of primarily white and non-immigrant students. Oscar reported that his peers were making hurtful comments about him, saying he did not "act" Guatemalan, that he was "too light skinned to really be an immigrant," and making jokes that he was "born in a jungle" and his family members in Guatemala were in gangs. Oscar felt that his few Latinx friends could not understand his feelings as they were all US-born. He described feeling tense, on edge, and alone while at school.

A month after the school counselor began helping Oscar process and express his feelings related to his immigrant status and microaggressions experienced at school, they received a call from Oscar's father. Oscar's father explained that they wanted the school counselor's guidance on how to break the news to Oscar that the family was not going to be renewing their green card and was planning on returning to Guatemala at the end of the school year. His father explained that over the last year, the family has felt increasingly unwelcome in the US due to their immigration status and were concerned about how the anti-immigrant climate in the country would get worse after the upcoming election. Oscar's father feared that Oscar would become upset with this news as he has spent his entire life in the US and considers it his home.

Reflection Questions

- How did the intersection between immigration status and race contribute to Oscar's distress?
- If you were the school counselor, how would you handle the father's request?
- Given the time limited nature of the counselor's work with Oscar, what do you believe the goals of treatment should be?
- How could the counselor advocate for Oscar's needs while at school?
- Do you see other areas for intervention beyond individual counseling?

immigrant and refugee students, create consultation circles, and teach staff how to sensitively navigate complex issues in the classroom. At the school level, practitioners can help advise administrators in the creation of group-based programs for immigrant students, school-wide socio-emotional lesson planning on xenophobia and prejudice, and can help create crisis plans for how to appropriately respond should there be issues of family separation, ICE raids, or deportation impacting a member of the school community. By educating, advocating, facilitating conversations, and connecting individuals to culturally responsive resources, practitioners can ensure that they establish the school as a safe place where immigrant and refugee students are seen and accepted.

Conclusion

As the population of immigrant and refugee students grows, so does the need for culturally attuned and responsive school-based supports. The painful intersection of immigration status and ethno-racial identity adds a complexity to the traumatic events that these students may face both at school and in the community. In order to create the appropriate interventions and services, clinicians must be aware of the unique and often distressing experiences that this population faces and the additional challenges that they face in receiving services. While this chapter acted as a general introduction to this population, we encourage those that work in areas with high immigrant populations to seek additional guidance in providing culturally responsive services.

References

Gonzales, R. G., Suarez-Orozco, C., & Dedios-Sanguineti, M. C. (2013). No place to belong: Contextualizing concepts of mental health among undocumented immigrant youth in the United States. *American Behavioral Scientist, 20*(10), 1–26.

Jaycox, L. G., Stein, B. D., Kataoka, S. H., Wong, M., Fink, A., Escudero, P., & Zaragoza, C. (2002). Violence exposure, posttraumatic stress disorder, and depressive symptoms among recent immigrant school children. *Journal of the American Academy for Child & Adolescent Psychiatry, 41*(9), 1104–1110.

Kim, I. (2016). Beyond trauma: Post-resettlement factors and mental health outcomes among Latino and Asian refugees in the United States. *Journal of Immigrant and Minority Health, 18*, 740–748.

Perez Foster, R. (2001). When immigration is trauma: Guidelines for the individual and family clinician. *American Journal of Orthopsychiatry, 71*(2), 153–170.

Segal, U. A., & Mayadas, N. S. (2005). Assessment of issues facing immigrant and refugee families. *Child Welfare, 74*(5), 563–583.

Racial Trauma and Play Therapy

14

Introduction

Play therapy is a treatment approach that emphasizes the therapeutic use of play to meet a child's emotional, behavioral, developmental, and relational needs (Drewes & Schaefer, 2010). It utilizes a child's natural form of communication to address psychosocial difficulties and facilitate growth in a developmentally appropriate way. Many children struggle with finding the exact words needed to describe their inner emotional world. However, with play, children do not need to speak to communicate. With this approach, toys represent a child's words and play represents their language (Landreth, 2012). In play therapy, children use toys and creative arts to express their thoughts, feelings, and experiences both literally and symbolically.

Play-based interventions can be extremely helpful for addressing school-related concerns. Specifically, it can be used to address adjustment to the classroom, teacher-student relationships, peer relationships, emotional and behavioral obstacles to learning, and disruptive behavior. Play can also be useful in providing group or classroom wide education on topics such as appropriate school behavior, social skills, academic skills, and self-regulation skills. Research on school-based play therapy has found a positive impact on student self-concept, internal locus of control, expressive language, classroom behavior problems, and the number of office referrals (Drewes & Schaefer, 2010). As school-based mental health professionals are tasked with meeting the diverse needs of the student body, they require a variety of approaches and interventions in their repertoire. Play therapy is noted as one of the most developmentally appropriate ways of meeting the socio-emotional and counseling needs of children at school (Drewes & Schaefer, 2010).

A benefit of using play in treatment is that it is atheoretical and appropriate with a wide range of populations. There are a variety of different approaches to play therapy including cognitive behavioral, narrative, child-centered, attachment-focused, Adlerian, and solution-focused. This treatment approach can be used across the age span, across developmental levels, and can be used to treat a variety of presenting concerns. As play therapy requires a much lower level of verbal communication than traditional talk therapy, it can be helpful when working with children struggling with racial stress and trauma.

Play Therapy and Racial Trauma

Play therapy is a therapeutic approach that is uniquely suited to meet the needs of children of color. Developmental research highlights how the developmental limitations in abstract thought and reasoning during childhood negatively impact a child's ability to understand concepts related to culture, identity, and race (Liu & Clay, 2002). Therefore, to address these issues in treatment, a therapeutic approach that mitigates these developmental challenges and provides a way for children of color to explore, understand, and make meaning of these concepts in a developmentally appropriate way is needed. Play is considered the universal language of children and has been identified as a natural and concrete way that children are able to communicate, express, and process their life experiences (Landreth, 2012). Additionally, research has found that play therapy is an effective tool used with children from culturally diverse groups (Drewes & Schaefer, 2010; Garza & Bratton, 2005). Play is appropriate for culturally diverse children because it represents a language that is present across ethnicities, exists in every language, and is utilized across the world. Thus, play therapy provides a culturally responsive way for children of color to reflect on their identity and the stressful experiences that may come with their group memberships.

As the therapeutic use of play in therapy is culturally responsive and appropriate for children of color, we argue that it also offers a useful way of meeting the needs of those struggling with racial trauma. After a traumatic event, children demonstrate a wide range of behaviors and ways of coping with their stress. Interestingly, one of the common responses to trauma that is observed in children is repetitive play, often related to circumstances of the trauma (Ogawa, 2004). As play is the natural language of children, research has consistently highlighted the effectiveness of play therapy as a treatment modality for children who have experienced a wide range of traumatic events (Drewes & Schaefer, 2010; Ogawa, 2004). After a traumatic event, play can help re-establish a sense of security, sense of control, and facilitate empowerment post-trauma.

We argue that due to this effectiveness with a wide range of traumas, play therapy can uniquely meet the needs of those struggling with racially traumatic experiences. While there is no current research that explicitly examines the use of play therapy with racial trauma, one study did examine the use of child-centered play therapy with traumatized refugee children. This study found that treatment was effective in reducing the amount of post-traumatic symptoms for children with cultural and community-related stress (Schottelkorb, et al., 2012). When a child experiences confusing, hurtful, and stressful experiences related to their cultural and racial group membership, they can experience a variety of trauma symptoms. These children struggle with finding the words to explain and make sense of aspects related to identity and have the additional difficulty of a diminished ability to express their feelings about their traumatic experiences. Accordingly, play provides a low pressure, non-verbal way to symbolically express the confusing and nuanced emotions that stem from racial injury and trauma.

Considerations for Play Therapy in a School Setting

Developmental Level of Student

Your approach to play therapy will vary depending on the age and developmental level of the student. Those that are working with pre-k to second-grade students may find that their "work" of counseling is heavily play and art-based with a primary emphasis on non-verbal communication. Students this young may not utilize a lot of talking in session and may feel more comfortable playing out or creating art work about scenarios rather than talking about them. Clinicians working with students in third through fifth grade may find that counseling is a balance of play, games, art, and some direct verbal communication. Students in this age group may be able to talk openly about their difficulties for short periods of time; however, when dysregulated or dealing with stressful topics, they may find symbolic play more comfortable. Lastly, clinicians working with students in middle school and high school may find that their therapy approach may have talking as the primary intervention with elements of play and creativity (e.g., structured games, art, music, etc.) supporting the student's exploration and expression.

Materials

Play-based interventions can be created and implemented using a variety of different materials. When determining what materials to use in session, clinicians should be mindful of the student's age, cognitive ability, sensory processing abilities, and level of risk. These factors can help determine if a specific material is appropriate for that student. For example, some students may demonstrate an aversion to soft and squishy sensations such as shaving cream or soap bubbles, while some may have a preference for sharp and spiky sensations such as with jacks, pine cones, and pin impression toys. With regards to risk level, if a student is unable to appropriately handle sharp objects such as scissors or is at risk of swallowing small items like Legos, then they may be avoided for safety purposes.

Toys and materials selected should facilitate a wide range of creative and emotional expression (Landreth, 2012). The clinician should ensure that the material selected can be easily manipulated by the student and does not require the student to be dependent on the adult for use. As play therapy emphasizes the child's autonomy and decision making in the room, the use of pre-programmed toys or electronic video games is not recommended (Landreth, 2012). These types of toys do not facilitate the child's creativity as the games and interactions are scripted. The following list is provided as an example of the type of materials and toys most commonly used for play therapy.

- Paper, paint, and clay
- Coloring utensils (e.g., crayons, markers, colored pencils, etc.)
- Magazines
- Egg cartons, shaving cream, feathers, pipe cleaners, and rocks
- Animal figures
- Dollhouse
- Family figures
- Masks
- Toy food and dishes
- Phones
- Cars and emergency vehicles
- Fake money
- Hand mirror
- Puppets
- Sandtray with miniatures
- Medical kit

- Dress up materials
- Baby doll
- Musical instruments
- Building blocks
- Aggressive toys (e.g., handcuffs, dart gun, plastic soldiers, etc.)

Basic Skills

When starting the journey of implementing play-based interventions into individual, group, or classroom interventions for racial trauma, the clinician is encouraged to practice and become familiar with the basic levels of interaction that are used in play therapy: mirroring, tracking, reflecting, and interpreting. These basic skills help build the therapeutic relationship, encourage feelings of safety, and facilitate growth (Landreth, 2012). Mirroring is when a clinician matches the child's affect, energy, and behavior in the therapy room. Mirroring demonstrates that the clinician is focusing on the student and reflecting back their experience in the moment. Mirroring can be demonstrated with the clinician's physical location, body language and posture, and behavior. By following the student around the room, positioning their body toward the student, and displaying similar facial expressions, the therapist is communicating that they hear them, they see them, they are allowing their lead, and they are interested in what the student is communicating (Landreth, 2012).

Tracking represents the therapist's verbal response to the child's actions and play expressions (Landreth, 2012). When a therapist is tracking a student's play behavior, they are putting into words what they are observing and acknowledging the student's non-verbal behavior. Some examples of tracking statements are "you are trying to decide what to play with first" and "you are pushing that right through there." Tracking helps the student feel the clinician is interested in their world and want to understand it (Landreth, 2012). When tracking, clinicians are discouraged from labeling an item before a student does, as it may be incorrect. For example, if a clinician observes a student knocking over a tower of blocks, a helpful non-labeling tracking statement would be "you are knocking that over!"

A therapist can reflect both the content of the child's expressions and the feelings behind those expressions. When reflecting content, the clinician summarizes or paraphrases what the student is expressing both verbally and symbolically (Landreth, 2012). This helps the student know that the clinician hears them, understands what they are communicating, and validates their perspective. Some examples of responses that reflect content are "you are wondering who was in there" and "no matter what they do, it is not enough to stop the tornado." When a clinician reflects feelings, they are communicating an understanding and acceptance of the student's feelings (Landreth, 2012). This facilitates the healthy understanding of emotional expression and encourages verbal communication. Some examples of statements that reflect feelings include "you are sad your friend moved" and "you did not like that and decided to find something else to play with."

The last skill of interpretation is when the clinician makes an interpretation about the character or object the student is using in their play. When making facilitative interpretations, the goal is to make a connection between the character/object/toy and the student. This can be communicated through direct or indirect statements. Depending on the theoretical approach you operate from, the use of interpretive statements may be encouraged or discouraged. For example, interpretation statements are considered inappropriate with a child-centered approach.

Practical Interventions

As described above, the use of play in therapy can be a powerful tool for working with traumatized children and can be helpful in addressing racial trauma. The creative activities described below offer opportunities for children and adolescents to process struggles related to race, ethnicity, identity, and stress through the use of play, art, and drama. They can be implemented in individual, group, and family settings.

Cultural Genogram

A helpful introduction activity that can be used to gather information about a child or adolescent's ethno-racial background is a cultural genogram. With the cultural genogram, a child creates a traditional three generation (or more) genogram; however, rather than focusing on family dynamics, the genogram focuses on cultural dynamics. The image created can provide useful information needed for treatment including their culture of origin, salient cultural identities, sources of pride and shame, and intergenerational trauma (Hardy & Laszloffy, 1995). The child can then create a key to represent migration patterns, languages used, early conditions of life in a new country, and experiences with discrimination, racism, xenophobia, and oppression. This genogram can also be used to identify the family and cultural significance of concepts like skin color, hair texture, language, religion, and level of assimilation

(Hardy & Laszloffy, 1995). This intervention can be implemented using a variety of modalities including drawing, collaging, and sand tray miniatures.

What Happens in Your House (or School)?

With this art intervention, children are invited to create a picture of their house with large windows to begin a discussion about the impact of stressful ethno-racial experiences on the family. It can be used to discuss community-level trauma, chronic trauma, or a single incident. In the windows, they are to tell stories about what kind of discussions or emotional responses are occurring inside the home related to community-level ethno-racial stressors. The image created by the child or adolescent can be used to discuss the differences between private and public reactions, how different family members cope with racial trauma, and the types of conversations their family is having. This intervention can also be used to discuss behaviors, reactions, and discussions held in the child's school. The windows to the classrooms can provide information about the child's perception of the school environment, teacher-student relationships, and peer interactions.

My Story

For many children and adolescents, imagery can act as a powerful tool to represent the feelings, thoughts, and beliefs they experience. As they may have difficulty finding the exact words to represent their experience, this intervention encourages the selection of cut out images to facilitate the disclosure of their life story. For this intervention, children are provided with a large selection of images (e.g., faces, locations, animals, items, words, etc.) and are invited to select as many as they need to tell their story. Clinicians should be mindful to select images that are culturally diverse and align with aspects of the child's life. This intervention can also be used in a variety of ways including talking about a specific incident, used for progress monitoring (how does their story change over time), and can be used during termination to reflect on their journey in treatment.

Trauma Trivia

In this psychoeducational game, the concept of ethno-racial stress and racial trauma is introduced to the young person in a fun and in-direct way. As with a typical game of trivia, the clinician creates categories and questions for the youth to answer and can assign points to each level of questions. Example categories can include general information about racial trauma, psychoeducation about post-traumatic symptoms, coping skills, and avenues of support. This game can be used to provide information and begin challenging the distortions a child may have about race, identity, and trauma. To reduce negative feelings around not knowing the "correct" answer, the clinician can offer an unlimited number of "helping hand" lifelines where the therapist can be called in to answer the question if the child is unsure of the answer.

Loss Pot

Grief and loss are common reactions that children and adolescents may have following a racially traumatic incident. They can struggle with a variety of losses including the loss of innocence, safety, relationships, and hope. Children are provided with a small terra cotta pot and are guided in safely breaking it into large pieces (3–5 pieces). They are then asked to write what they have lost, how they have changed post-incident, and how they feel about their loss on each piece. As the child processes and grieves their losses, together, the child and therapist work on gluing the pieces back together. Once the pieces are glued together to repair the pot, the child is invited to decorate and cover up their writings, plant seeds, and grow a plant to demonstrate how growth can come from loss.

Layers of Me

Older children may struggle with negative feelings regarding societal stereotypes and assumptions about aspects of their cultural identity. With this activity, tweens and teens can begin to make meaning around the ways that they contradict harmful stereotypes. Youth are invited to draw and cut out body outlines from three plastic freezer bags to create a see-through self-image. On the top layer, the young person writes about the assumptions that society makes about them based on their personal attributes (e.g., looks, group membership, family, community, etc.). On the middle layer, positive traits they have that combat these assumptions and stereotypes are written. On the bottom layer, core feelings about and reactions to these assumptions and microaggressions that the youth keeps hidden from others are listed. The cutouts are then stapled together at the top and the image produced is used to guide reflection on group memberships, societal issues, meaning making, sources of support, and coping.

Cultural Wealth

To help empower, identify strengths, and build resilience post-trauma, children and adolescents are invited to create a piggy bank to symbolize their cultural wealth. This piggy bank can be created out of a variety of materials including a box, cup, bottle, and balloon. After decorating their piggy bank, the child creates coins and dollar bills that have positive aspects of their identity written on them. This activity can be used to highlight how their cultural identity is something to be celebrated and facilitate discussion about how their culture makes them rich. Some examples of empowering statements include:

- My hair is coily and healthy
- I speak two languages
- I am culturally unique
- My ancestors were survivors
- My skin is brown and beautiful
- I have lived in several countries
- My culture's traditions are meaningful

I Am Not My Trauma

In this experiential art activity, tweens and teens cover a large picture of themselves with a piece of saran wrap and affix it to a piece of poster board. While looking at the picture, they are encouraged to name positive traits about themselves and their cultural identity. The therapist then guides the youth in throwing different colored paints at the picture to symbolize the negative messages or events that they have received or experienced because of their ethno-racial identity. As they process how they feel about the covered picture and relate it to their positive and negative feelings about their identity, the therapist removes the saran wrap to reveal a pristine picture. Together, the pair reflects on how the messages and events do not change their amazing, unique, and authentic core self.

Resilience Rucksack

The last practical intervention provided is appropriate for termination, as children create a bag or box that can be used to help them manage and survive racial injury and trauma in the future. The emphasis of the intervention is on thinking about and practicing how to apply the knowledge and skills to reduce future distress. Through art, children are encouraged to create a box or rucksack that can be a go-to coping resource. The items included in the rucksack should be tailored to the youth's interests, cultural identity, and developmental level. A list of helpful items to include are:

- Healthy coping tools (e.g., sensory items, grounding tools, art supplies, etc.)
- A note card on potential trauma triggers and a coping plan
- Positive, hopeful, and empowering quotes, images, and symbols that stem as reminders of therapy
- Items or artwork created during treatment
- A post-crisis plan for how to reconnect with themselves, their family, their peers, and their community after a race-related crisis

Conclusion

The use of play-based interventions in treatment is a developmentally and culturally appropriate treatment approach for meeting the needs of children of color who are struggling with their exposure to racially traumatic experiences. This approach can be used in a variety of different ways including individually, in a group, and classroom wide. Play can allow these children to speak about the unspeakable and provides an opportunity to sensitively address their difficulty without the pressure of finding the right words to describe their experience. The therapeutic use of play can also provide fun and exciting ways for children to do the work of talk therapy in a way that builds insight, boosts resilience, and prepares them for future challenges. We strongly encourage school-based clinicians to consider adding this evidence-based treatment modality into their toolbox of interventions.

References

Drewes, A.A., & Schaefer, C.E. (2010). *School-based play therapy* (2nd ed.). John Wiley & Sons, Inc.

Garza, Y., & Bratton, S.C. (2005). School-based child-centered play therapy with Hispanic children: Outcomes and cultural considerations. *International Journal of Play Therapy, 14,* 51–80.

Hardy, K.V., & Laszloffy, T.A. (1995). The cultural genogram: Key to training culturally competent family therapists. *Journal of Marital and Family Therapy, 21*(3), 227–237.

Landreth, G.L. (2012). *Play therapy: The art of the relationship* (3rd ed.). Routledge.

Liu, W., & Clay, D.L. (2002). Multicultural counseling competencies: Guidelines in working with children and adolescents. *Journal of Mental Health Counseling, 24*(2), 177–189.

Ogawa, Y. (2004). Childhood trauma and play therapy intervention for traumatized children. *Journal of Professional Counseling: Practice, Theory & Research, 32*(1), 19–29.

Schottelkorb, A.A., Doumas, D.M., & Garcia, R. (2012). Treatment for childhood refugee trauma: A randomized, controlled trial. *International Journal of Play Therapy, 21*(2), 57–73.

Racial Trauma and Bibliotherapy

15

Introduction

Storytelling is the art of sharing narratives and stories as a means of expression, entertainment, education, relationship building, and cultural preservation. Historically, storytelling has been an important practice in Black and Indigenous communities as oral stories have been used to preserve cultural knowledge and practices that have been lost through colonization. During times of slavery, storytelling also held an important cultural significance as it provided opportunities for the enslaved to experience respite, joy, and be seen as more than property. Across generations, stories have been used as a coping tool during times of stress and trauma, to express feelings, provide validation, and make meaning. The therapeutic use of books in therapy, known as bibliotherapy, taps into the use of storytelling to help children understand their problems and how to make meaning from their experiences.

This chapter provides an overview of how to utilize books as a therapeutic intervention for students experiencing stressful race-related experiences. Information on the goals of bibliotherapy, the traditional four-step approach, and research on the psychological benefits will be provided. Guidelines for how to integrate books into the classroom and the therapy room will be discussed, as well as information on how a clinician can use bibliotherapy to augment their trauma interventions. Lastly, a selection of useful books that can be used with children and adolescents who are struggling with traumatic ethno-racial experiences will be reviewed.

Bibliotherapy and Racial Trauma

The term bibliotherapy was first used in the early 20th century to describe the use of books for psychological healing (Davis et al., 2017). It refers to the therapeutic technique of using books to help children learn from and cope with their life experiences. Books can provide children with an avenue to explore a variety of worlds, real and imagined. In bibliotherapy, the hope is that children will see themselves reflected in the stories chosen, allowing them to approach their problems in a non-threatening way. Stories can provide youth with support for a variety of social, emotional, behavioral, and developmental concerns. As many children have difficulty finding the words to explain their experience, stories can provide youth with a narrative around a common problem in a developmentally appropriate way. This technique can be used flexibly, either in a proactive way or in response to a stressor. Bibliotherapy can also be used across a variety of environments including classrooms, individual therapy, and group therapy (Davis et al., 2017).

Research on children's literacy has shown a consistent gap in the racial and ethnic makeup of the books made for children. The Cooperative Children's Book Center (CCBC) examined the diversity gap in US publishing and found that in the year 2019 out of 3,717 books received, 12% of books featured Black characters, 9% featured Asian characters, 6% featured Latinx characters, 2% featured Indigenous characters, 1% featured Arab characters, and .001% featured Pacific Islander characters (2020). The CCBC also found that in 2019, only 23% of children's books received were published by BIPOC authors (Cooperative Children's Book Center, 2020). Unfortunately, the reality in the US is that children of color rarely have books that mirror their identity due to a shortage in diverse and multicultural books. Even less are the books that are specifically focused on race and ethnicity. This means that many of these children are not shown stories that help them feel seen, heard, and validated in their experiences.

Since children of color are not often shown stories that feature characters that look like them, the purposeful and mindful integration of books for therapeutic use in therapy can be extremely powerful. For some children, experiencing the therapy room (and the materials in it) as reflective of their reality in a positive way can be a significant corrective emotional experience. Bibliotherapy is a useful intervention for addressing racial trauma as it offers a structured, sensitive, and indirect way to introduce painful experiences and topics into conversation. As with any trauma, finding out how to approach details of the traumatic event in a way that does not re-traumatize the child can be difficult. Added difficulty is also seen with chronic community-based trauma, such as racial trauma, as it becomes a part of the child's daily reality.

Research has shown that bibliotherapy is a successful intervention with children exposed to chronic trauma in the community as it helps promote feelings of security, alleviates fears, and allows them to temporarily escape the stress of their daily experience (De Vries et al., 2017). Additionally, with racial injury and trauma, the experience of talking about the trauma is complicated by the added social punishment that people of color experience for disclosing (Williams et al., 2018). With bibliotherapy, the use of books in fun and positive ways can help take the pressure out of the disclosure and demonstrate that it is a safe space to process it.

Using books in therapy that feature racially diverse characters can also help children of color to feel empowered. So many children receive hurtful and confusing messages related to their ethno-racial identity through the media and daily microaggressions experienced in the community. As described in a previous chapter, these types of negative messages have the impact to negatively alter a child's identity development, leading to negative mental health outcomes. Bibliotherapy can use stories to provide contrasting positive narratives regarding topics like skin color, culture, hair texture, language, and migration status. In stories, children can see how characters of color are presented in ways that defy stereotypes, emphasize the positive aspects of being culturally unique, and instill feelings of pride, joy, and resilience.

The Four Steps of Bibliotherapy

Identification

The first step in the bibliotherapy process is identification, where the goal is to help the child identify with the characters presented in the story (Heath et al., 2005). To facilitate this process, the clinician must be purposeful about finding a book that aligns with the child's identity. While it may not be possible to find characters that perfectly match a child, it is important that they are similar in age, gender, race, language, and circumstance. While many children's books feature animal characters, given the importance of identity in issues of racial trauma, emphasis should be put on finding books with human characters.

Catharsis

Once a book is selected, the next step is catharsis. Catharsis refers to the process by which a child becomes emotionally involved in the story. They put themselves in the shoes of the character and identify with their struggles. During this experience, children begin to recognize and indirectly experience the character's feelings (Heath et al., 2005). This can help facilitate the release of pent-up feelings in a safe and validating environment. By identifying with the characters and becoming invested in the story, youth begin to see solutions to their problems.

Insight

The third step in the bibliotherapy process is insight, which represents the youth's connection of the story to their life. After they have read the story, they begin thinking about what happened in the story, the way problems were solved, and begin to apply it to their own situation (Heath et al., 2005). During this process, they are able to see how the characters were capable of change, growth, and positive outcomes, which helps them see that as a possibility for themselves.

Universalization

Lastly, universalization represents a child's realization that their problems are not unique and they are not alone. During this point, they feel supported and are able to gain a broader perspective (Davis, et al., 2017; Heath et al., 2005). Upon reaching this step, children experience emotional relief and are able to view their situation and their future with a new lens of hope and understanding. With this new lens, they are able to use coping skills, try out new behavior, and tap into their personal strengths moving forward (Davis et al., 2017; Heath et al., 2005).

The Process of Bibliotherapy

Planning

When deciding to use bibliotherapy for children who have a history of racially traumatic experiences, mindful planning is needed to ensure the intervention is appropriate and effective. First, the clinician should ensure that they have a thorough understanding of the child's presenting problem to facilitate the selection of relevant books. Next, reflecting on the goals of treatment is important (Davis et al., 2017). Specifically, what is the main focus of treatment? What skills does the child need to work on? What is the most urgent area for intervention? Additionally, reflecting on the child's cognitive ability and reading level occurs during the planning stage to help guide future book selection.

The clinician must also assess the youth's readiness to discuss their problems (De Vries et al., 2017). This assessment is necessary as it can help determine whether you need to select a book that explicitly discusses their struggles or is loosely related. This is particularly important when working with trauma as those who are highly traumatized may not wish to speak directly about their stressful experiences. If a youth is open, ready, and comfortable talking about their trauma, books with direct messages may be helpful to use. However, if they are avoidant, reluctant, or easily distressed, then selecting a series of books that start very broad and slowly narrow in focus may be a more appropriate approach.

Book Selection

Once you have reflected on the child, their presentation, and their appropriateness for bibliotherapy, your focus should switch to book selection. In order for bibliotherapy to be effective and promote change, the books selected must align with the child's current difficulties (Davis et al., 2017). We strongly emphasize that clinicians review all books prior to using them. This review of the story will ensure that the clinician is familiar with the story, the images, and the message put forth by the author. In doing so, the clinician is able to anticipate potential areas for discussion. To help guide your careful selection of bibliotherapy material, the following reflection questions are provided:

- What is the story about?
- What language is it in?
- What kind of characters are featured?
- What do the characters look like? Are they realistic? Are they culturally similar to the child?
- Are characters presented positively or negatively?
- What developmental level is this book appropriate for?
- What reading level does this book require?
- Does the book include any of the child's interests?
- Are the images calming or do they evoke strong emotion?
- Does the story depict any sensitive topics?
- Is the book relevant to the child's current situation?
- Does the book contain any trauma triggers?

- Does the story provide comfort and reassurance regarding the situation?
- What is the ultimate message that the author is conveying?

Implementation

After planning and selecting the appropriate book, the last step is to implement the intervention and share the story with the child or adolescent. Some children will request to read the books themselves, some will request the clinician read the story, and some do best with alternating reading between therapist and child. While reading the story, intentional reflection questions can be used to help the child connect with the story. Once the book has been read, clinicians should gather information about the child's experience of the story. A specific focus should be paid to the child's connection to the characters and their journey. Lastly, purposeful discussion questions can be used to process the story, which can help children enter the insight and universalization stages. For those that struggle with verbal expression, artwork can be a very helpful modality in expressing thoughts, feelings, and reactions to the story in a safe and non-threatening way.

Book Recommendations for Racial Trauma

Figuring out what books to start with can be overwhelming when building your library for bibliotherapy. The categories and books listed below are provided as examples of the types of books that can be helpful when working stressful ethno-racial experiences in therapy.

Cultural Differences

- *I'm like you, you're like me* (Gainer, 2013)
- *What is your language?* (Leventhal, 1994)
- *My family, your family* (Bullard, 2015)
- *Same, same but different* (Kostecki-Shaw, 2011)
- *Black is a rainbow color* (Joy, 2020)
- *The proudest blue: A story of hijab and family* (Muhammad & Ali, 2019)
- *This book is anti-racist: 20 lessons on how to wake up, take action, and do the work* (Jewell, 2020)
- *Where are you from?* (Saied Mendez, 2019)

Skin Color

- *Shades of Black* (Pinkney, 2006)
- *Skin like mine* (Perry, 2016)
- *Hey Black child* (Perkins, 2019)
- *All the colors we are* (Kissinger, 2014)
- *The colors of us* (Katz, 2002)
- *Black is brown is tan* (Adoff, 2004)

Positive Self-image

- *I love my hair* (Tarpley, 2001)
- *I am enough* (Byers, 2018)
- *Beautiful, wonderful, strong little me!* (Carmona Dias, 2019)
- *I believe I can* (Byers, 2020)
- *Hair love* (Cherry, 2019)
- *All because you matter* (Charles, 2020)

Historical and Community Trauma

- *Something happened in our town* (Celano et al., 2019)
- *Busing Brewster* (Michelson, 2019)
- *The hate u give* (Thomas, 2017)
- *Brown girl dreaming* (Woodson, 2016)
- *Dear Martin* (Stone, 2018)
- *The Black kids* (Hammonds Reed, 2020)
- *Woke: A young poet's call to justice* (Browne, et al., 2020)
- *We are water protectors* (Lindstrom, 2020)
- *I am not a number* (Kay Dupuis & Kacer, 2016)

Immigrant and Refugee

- *Two white rabbits* (Buitrago, 2015)
- *I hate English!* (Levine, 1995)
- *The name jar* (Choi, 2003)
- *Dreamers* (Morales, 2018)
- *I'm new here* (O'Brien, 2018)

- *My family divided: One girls' journey of home, loss, and hope* (Guerrero & Moroz, 2019)
- *Americanized: Rebel without a green card* (Saedi, 2019)
- *Mama's nightingale: A story of immigration and separation* (Danticat, 2015)

Case Example: Kailani

Kailani is a fourth-grade bi-racial student who was born in Hawai'i but was raised in Georgia. Her mother was a native Hawaiian, while her father is Black. Kailani's mother died at birth and she has lived with her paternal family her entire life. Given her mixed background, Kailani's skin color is noticeably lighter than her father's and she is often described as "ethically ambiguous." During her toddler years, there had been several incidents where the police were called on her father in public, as bystanders did not believe that Kailani was his daughter.

Luz, the school social worker, began having 2×/week check-ins with Kailani after she participated in an afterschool social skills group. She was initially referred to the group as she was struggling to make friends and was socially anxious. Luz noticed that after the 6-week group had ended, Kailani was still struggling with her school relationships and was disconnected from adults. After Kailani struggled to engage in the check-ins, Luz conducted a home visit to build her relationship with Kailani's father and assess whether the family needed any support with stressors in the home. During the home visit, Kailani's father informed Luz that he is concerned about her interactions with her extended family. He noticed that Kailani is ignored by her cousins and seems anxious around her aunts and uncles.

The next week Luz decides to try using bibliotherapy with Kailani to help her open up. At her check-in, Luz explains to Kailani that she needs help organizing her book collection and asks if she would like to help. Kailani excitedly agrees and begins to look through the different books available. Luz notices that Kailani has stopped and is staring at the books that feature diverse families. Luz shows her a book with bi-racial siblings on the front and explains that this is a new book that she has never read before and invites Kailani to read it with her.

As Kailani is reading the book, she touches the page and whispers "his skin is light like mine, but his sister is darker … like my dad." When they finish the story, Kailani asks Luz if they can read it again. After they read the book a second time, Luz suggested that they draw themselves. As Kailani is coloring, she begins talking about her parents and how they had different skin colors like the parents in the story. She also explained that her aunts and uncles make confusing comments about her looks, which upsets her cousins as they feel like

Kailani is the favorite. She then explained that in school, she has trouble fitting in because she does not know who to hang out with. Kailani became frustrated with her drawing, balling it up and throwing it across the room. She crossed her arms and said "My dad says I'm Black, but my friends are confused because my skin is golden. I don't get it."

Reflection Questions

- How do you conceptualize Kailani's struggles?
- What treatment goals would you recommend?
- What additional information would you like to know about Kailani?
- Do you feel like the use of a book was helpful or hurtful? Why?
- What types of books may be helpful to use with Kailani in the future?
- Would you have done anything different?

References

Adoff, A. (2004). *Black is Brown is tan* (E.A. Mcully, Illus.). HarperCollins.

Browne, M.L., Acevedo, E., & Gatwood, O. (2020). *Woke: A young poet's call to justice* (T. Taylor, Illus.). Roaring Brook Press.

Buitrago, J. (2015). *Two white rabbits* (R. Yockteng, Illus.). Groundwood Books.

Bullard, L. (2015). *My family, your family* (R. Kurilla, Illus.). Millbrook Press.

Byers, G. (2018). *I am enough* (K.A. Bobo, Illus.). Balzer and Bray.

Byers, G. (2020). *I believe I can* (K.A. Bobo, Illus.). Balzer and Bray.

Carmona Dias, H. (2019). *Beautiful, wonderful, strong little me!* (D. Georgieva-Goda, Illus.). Eifrig Publishing.

Celano, M., Collins, M., & Hazard, A. (2019). *Something happened in our town* (J. Zivoin, Illus.). Magination Press.

Charles, T. (2020). *All because you matter* (B. Collier, Illus.). Orchard Books.

Cherry, M. A. (2019). *Hair love* (V. Harrison, Illus.). Kokila.

Choi, Y. (2003). *The name jar.* Dragonfly Books.

Cooperative Children's Book Center. (2020, October 27). *Children's books by and/or about Black, indigenous, and people of color received by the CCBC-U.S. Publishers only 2018–2019.* Cooperative Children's Book Center, School of Education, University of Wisconsin-Madison.https://ccbc.education.wisc.edu/literature-resources/ccbc-diversity-statistics/books-by-and-or-about-poc-2018/#USonly.

Danticat, E. (2015). *Mama's nightingale: A story of immigration and separation* (L. Staub, Illus.). Dial Books.

Davis, A.P., Wilcoxon, S.A., & Townsend, K.M. (2017). Options and considerations for using bibliotherapy in the school setting. *The Alabama Counseling Association Journal, 41*(2), 65–81.

De Vries, D., Brennan, Z., Lankin, M., Morse, R., Rix, B., & Beck, T. (2017). Healing with books: A literature review of bibliotherapy used with children and youth who have experience trauma. *Therapeutic Recreation Journal, 51*(1), 48–74.

Gainer, C. (2013). *I'm like you, you're like me: A book about understanding and appreciating each other* (M. Sakamoto, Illus.). Free Spirit Publishing.

Guerrero, D., & Moroz, E. (2019). *My family divided: One girl's journey of home, loss, and hope*. Square Fish.

Hammonds Reed, C. (2020). *The Black kids*. Simon & Schuster Books for Young Readers.

Heath, M.A., Sheen, D., Leavy, D., Young, E., & Money, K. (2005). Bibliotherapy: A resource to facilitate emotional healing and growth. *School Psychology International, 26*(5), 563–580.

Jewell, T. (2020). *This book is anti-racist: 20 lessons on how to wake up, take action, and do the work* (A. Durand, Illus.). Frances Lincoln Children's Books.

Joy, A. (2020). *Black is a rainbow color* (E. Holmes, Illus.). Roaring Brook Press.

Katz, K. (2002*). The colors of us*. Square Fish.

Kay Dupuis, J., & Kacer, K. (2016). *I am not a number* (G. Newland, Illus.). Second Story Press.

Kissinger, K. (2014). *All the color we are: The story of how we got our skin color*. Redleaf Press.

Kostecki-Shaw, J.S. (2011). *Same, same but different*. Henry Holt and co.

Leventhal, D. (1994). *What is your language?* (M. Wellington, Illus.). Dutton Juvenile.

Levine, E. (1995). *I hate English!* (S. Bjorkman, Illus.). Scholastic Paperbacks.

Lindstrom, C. (2020). *We are water protectors* (M. Goade, Illus.). Roaring Book Press.

Michelson, R. (2019). *Busing brewster* (R.G. Roth, Illus.). David R. Godine, Publisher.

Morales, Y. (2018). *Dreamers*. Neal Porter Books.

Muhammad, I., & Ali, S.K. (2019). *The proudest blue: A story of hijab and family* (H. Aly, Illus.). Little, Brown Books for Young Readers.

O'Brien, A.S. (2018). *I'm new here*. Charlesbridge.

Perkins, U.E. (2019). *Hey Black child* (B. Collier, Illus.). LB Kids.

Perry, L.M. (2016). *Skin like mine*. G Publishing.

Pinkney, S.L. (2006). *Shades of Black: A celebration of our children* (M. Pinkney, Illust.). Cartwheel Books.

Saedi, S. (2019). *Americanized: Rebel without a green card*. Ember.

Saied Mendez, Y. (2019). *Where are you from?* (J. Kim, Illus.). HarperCollins.

Stone, N. (2018). *Dear Martin*. Ember.

Tarpley, N.A. (2001). *I love my hair!* (E.B. Lewis, Illus.). Little, Brown Books for Young Readers.

Thomas, A. (2017). *The hate u give*. Balzer and Bray.

Williams, M.T., Metzger, I.W., Leins, C., & DeLapp, C. (2018). Assessing racial trauma within a DSM–5 framework: The UConn Racial/Ethnic stress & trauma survey. *Practice Innovations, 3*(4), 242–260.

Woodson, J. (2016). *Brown girl dreaming*. Puffin Books.

Index

Note: Folios in **boldface** indicate tables in the text.

Made in United States
Orlando, FL
22 March 2022

16005874R20085